Skinhead... The Life I Chose

Spike Pitt

Skinhead: The Life I Chose

Spike Pitt

longshanks_98@yahoo.com

Published by Bronwyn Editions 2016 UK
ISBN:978-0-9570745-9-0

Cover design by D M Samson

Introduction

This is a true account of the skinhead cult, told by a man who was really there and still is. It is NOT about Nazism, or Neo-Nazism, and definitely not about politics; it is the story of how the ebullience of youth can be corrupted and misinterpreted by propaganda and the media.

Warning

This story contains a lot of strong language, British slang and outspoken opinions that may be offensive to some; it is nevertheless the truth.

In uniform with sister, Tania

Acknowledgements

I just want to thank my Wife and Family for putting up with me; my Granddaughter for giving me so much Joy; my poor old Mum who put up with so much shit from me and Dan as young Skins. For the endless lines of Punks and Skins through the house; all my real friends who have stayed loyal, for the bands and songs that have given me fun and excitement; to all Skins, Punks and Mods for keeping the cults going.

A big fuck off to the media and politicians for their deception and lies, and last, but not least, thanks to Bernie, Dave Samson and Bronwyn Editions; without her and the help none of this would have been done: REAL people without any deception. Told you many times, B, LOVE YOU... SKINHEAD.

Skinhead: The Life I Chose

How to start... My name: well, it's really Russell, but people know me as Spike, and these chapters are how I remember them. They are memories around the skinhead cult of the late 70s until now; Punks, Mods, and others are here. I'm not going to put everything in precise date order as some events and time-line are hard to completely put together. Some things I say may not be agreeable to everyone, as the truth will hurt, but they're from my own experience and how I feel.

Certain names I have changed, as people change and some don't want to be associated with things that went on. However, those whose real names or nicknames used, have given their full permission, with pride.

These are my personal memoirs. I was there: good or bad, laughs, politics, music and a feeling of belonging. There is no politically correct rubbish – this is how it was. It's not the like the film, *This Is England* {What was that about REALLY!} made for nostalgia?

Spike Pitt

The Sounds

The music Skins listen to since the late 70s has not changed that much. I don't follow a lot of the Oi bands now, but there probably still are a few. I don't think Skin will ever lose its roots with Ska and Trojan, Bluebeat, or even Two-tone. I hope not, as they're all great to dance to, and, of course, there is *Slade*. How can any Skin not take notice of them? I do go to a lot of Mod nights as some of the DJs play a lot of Ska, et al, so that keeps me and my son happy (bloody Mod). There was a good Ska music scene in Reading not so long ago: plenty of older Skins coming along to have a laugh, drink and dance, but the Skin who used to do the music has since moved away with his wife to France (Paul and Anna). The lucky French Skins now have that pleasure of their endless supply of Ska, Bluebeat, and Skinhead Reggae to fill them with joy.

For me, I'll just keep going to see Reading's, NO Berkshire's, NO EVEN THE WHOLE SOUTH'S best pub band: *The Highwasters*. Plenty of Punk, Skin, Rock, Mod, and other music to completely give us a great night's entertainment.

Kids 1968

My earliest memory is of the original Skins...

The first time I ever saw those who became known as skinheads was through my elder brother, Bob (rest in peace, mate). We were living in an old police station in London and the cells were still there downstairs. He and his mates were let in there by Mum and Dad, to use as their meeting place and my younger bro and me used to sneak down to listen and try to get involved, a slap around the head often taken.

"Piss off Russ and Dan or get a boot up the arse!" was a regular sound heard, and also me and Dan running away, pleading for help from Mum and Dad. Bob and his friends were some of the early Skins; the Mod thing was too expensive for them they would say, and we, as a family, never had a lot of money. We were what people would class as poor, and also going to footy in a suit is not a good idea, he used to say.

I suppose the times were changing in England, and especially in the big towns and cities of the time. New music: Ska, Blue beat and skinhead Reggae was about. Well, it had been around for ages, but the people who all became Skins were clubbing to that sound and the dress by now was in place.

All had number two hair cuts; there was only one of Bob's mates who had a number 1, and all had sideburns. It was great to see them all polishing the boots (Doc Martens and Monkey boots) before going out – a nice Brutus checked shirt (or Ben Sherman), also Fred Perry polo shirts. The jeans were Levis, but I'm sure there were Wranglers {my favourite as a Skin} as well. Some would have Harrington jackets on; others, if a little colder, donkey jackets, Crombie, and sheepskin coats.

I can always remember one of Bob's mates had a full length

sheepskin; how he moved in a fight I'll never know, and he was the first person I saw with a Mohican {long time before the Punks}. He grew it about an inch in height and the back bit of the Mohican he left growing {this was about 1970} and it hung down in a straight line until it reached his shoulder blades. It looked like a hoplite Greek Helmet, and I never did see him in his party clothes, never ever had his own two-tone or sta-press suit. Bob and the others always used to take the piss, but must admit they'd lend him some clothes to party with at times.

It was always good to see what colour suit they would put on, or sta-press, what colour the braces were, boots for the day, shoes on if going clubbing {disco then}. Loafers, brogues, were the ones I always saw worn, again highly polished, also a flat cap was worn by a few − it seemed popular. I cannot remember seeing a pork pie hat worn. Bob did have a flat cap and a trilby and I think one of his mates had a trilby as well, but I was only nine in '69 so I could be wrong.

Another item of use, or not as the case may show, was the comb; quite a few Skins {blokes} had one. I never knew why; grade 2 to 4 haircut didn't really need a comb but there it was, probably a thing left over from the Mod culture from which we came. You would never ever see a Mod without a comb; it's just not done − like fish and chips with no salt and vinegar, but I must say I've always carried one.

Cardigans and tank tops were also a much worn item, and I have many to this day, but glad to say I've never had the multi-coloured ones {tank tops} the Suedeheads wore − that's going too far. Tie pins in the Crombie breast pocket with a hanky, white or red. I can only remember those colours, possibly others, but those are the ones that stay in the mind. Bob also wore a tie pin in his suit breast pocket − a thing I still do today, smart as fuck.

I didn't see too many skingirls: WRENS, they were called by Bob and co, but Mum and Dad didn't let many girls in, "DON'T WANT NO FUCKING BLOKE COMING ROUND HERE SAYING YOU GOT HIS GIRL UP THE DUFF". Understandable, Dad. About the girls of that time I can only remember their short skirts and short dresses; it was still Mod influenced in style. I just can't remember seeing them in boots – they may have worn them, but the memory fades. Even at that young age Dan and I would sneak peek at those legs and vie to see who saw the knickers first.

Again I cannot remember them wearing braces. I did see a few girls in Sherman and Brutus shirts, and also Fred Perry, but please don't quote me. I also saw some girls in a sheepskin and Crombie, and then there was the haircut: THE FEATHER. Or like Mum would say, "That's not a feather cut". Got to admit, back in the 60s and early 70s some of the girls did not always have what is seen now as the skingirl hair cut – the cut of grade 4 {and shorter if wanted} on top and the fringes on the front, sides and back left to grow. Some just had short hair, some had what was called the Pixie cut, I think, but anyway a tad different to the Wrens nowadays.

I can remember the turn-ups for the jeans being done and it looked funny seeing the girls in a cell doing turn-ups for the lads. Bob always said, "Get these girls working – could earn a mint", and those turn-ups had to be quarter or half inch stitched just right, or the sta-press taken up to the correct height: turn-up on the inside for them and the suit trousers.

These images were great and on top of that the music. Yeah things are different now; Skins can listen to main stream Punk, or the stuff they called Oi {silly name}. I like to call it street Punk, as well as 2tone {which I hate} and the original Ska, and that's where my introduction to the music of Ska, and *Laurel Aitken*, first took hold of me. Of all the groups, singers, et al, of that time, Mr Aitken is the one I remember the most; he was for me Mr Skinhead tunes. I never ever got to see Bob and the crew at disco's – too young, so never got to see all the dancing, and listen to all the other groups they danced to, and there were many.

Often Bob and co were told to "TURN THAT BLOODY CRAP OFF, IT'S NOT JAMAICA HERE!" Dad had a way with words, but he didn't like to admit that he and Mum often secretly moved their feet to the beat. Dan and I sometimes caught them.

There also was a lot of violence, for Bob, he could handle himself, and his mates were all good with the other side of the skinhead scene: aggro but, during the 60s and early 70s, it wasn't a racial thing. I cannot remember any – well, no one ever said anything about racial violence.

It was funny to see police at the house – an old police station – after Bob, usually because of something that happened in the disco the night before, or that he and the crew had attacked some hippies or had a dust-up with some other Skins from somewhere else, and I can remember Bob and co with some black Skins going Paki-bashing. Can you imagine that now?

I didn't hear about footy violence in the late 60s or early 70s, probably because the media didn't make such a big thing of it, but Bob and co had to be up to something on footy days. Those years between '68 and '73 Bob was a Skin and I saw the police a lot, involving him, and on one occasion the violence that took place changed my view of the police forever. Yes, they do a hard job, but sometimes that uniform does not give them the right to give people beatings, knowing their uniform protects them.

Bob and some of his mates had pinched some cigarettes and someone who saw them knew and told the police who it was. It had been an open season on Bob and the crew, so it was just the excuse for the police to raid the house. Needless to say, they came in force with violent bursting through the front door and chasing Bob into the back yard. While doing so, had knocked my Mum to the floor which one paid for a few minutes later. They caught Bob in the garden with his mates.

Dan and I were cleaning out the rabbits. Dad kept them for show and meat {which was still eaten then}. All we heard was "You skinhead barstards – got you, you're nicked." Then really laid into them. Well Dan and I saw red; being nine and ten years of age didn't stop us. We charged the plod closest to us. In my haste I attacked a police officer with a carrot, yep a carrot, and then saw my Mum all four foot ten of her charge the plod with fist clenched, gritted teeth and that Geordie accent going mental, towards the one who had put her to the floor. WALLOP! a right cross followed by punches and combinations Henry Cooper would have been proud of.

Bob and his mate were beaten and taken away. Mum was nicked and Dad had to come home from work to collect Dan and me and also our little sis who was a baby. This did change Dan's and my feelings towards the police. I'm not saying they are all bad, but trust them, NO, and if it comes to a bit of violence, get in first before they mob up and do you, eye for an eye.

Bob finally stopped being Skin in about '73; he didn't even go through the suede thing; he went from one extreme to another. He got involved with Hell's Angels and the use of drugs {I hate drugs with a passion} and the use of these accelerated the terminal brain disease that is cursed upon our family: Huntington's disease took him at an early age, but those memories of his skinhead days will always stay with me, and probably what subconsciously made Dan and me skinheads for so long.

The Clobber Now

Before I go into more memories from the old loaf, let's see how the skinhead scene had changed, what happened and how it changed me.

Clothes: well things had not changed too much except the boots had got higher than the 8 and 10 holes from the late 60s; now we had DMs of 12 or 14 hole and there even was a pair with 20 holes – very silly. The jeans were worn higher up the leg, showing more boot than in the original days, just because of the boot getting taller and it looked meaner. Ox blood and black DMs were the two boot colours – none of this stupid red or multi-colour shite you have nowadays. How to ruin a good pair of boots, but kids today haven't got a clue. We also wore a pair of 12 eye-hole steel toecap boots. They weren't Docs {even though Docs made a good pair of steels} and I can't remember their real name – not like DMs – they didn't have a soft sole, but a solid bottom that looked really nasty. They were a good pair of boots, but heavy. We always got them from the *Army & Navy Stores*; they were about £30 I think, but it was 1977-78-79-80s and that was a lot of money then.

Shoes were the same: loafers or brogues, black and ox blood colours, and Doc Marten also made a shoe that got popular; I had a few pairs. Most Skins wore braces, although there were a few who didn't. We always wore what became known as 1/2 inch wide braces. But I never did measure to see how wide they were and still are, and now you can get ¼ inch braces and there are multi-colours to choose from.

Shirts: *Brutus* and *Ben Sherman*. I also used to wear and still do, granddad collar shirts and Penny collar shirts. It just looked good; a bit of improvisation didn't look too bad and it caught on. *Fred Perry* polo tops were still very popular and, there again, many colours to choose from, but I must say I didn't really like Fred Perry – it was just too Mod for me. Also printed T-shirts were worn a lot, bands you followed or Union Jack, St George flag or wherever you were from. Football shirts as well made up the wardrobe. I even saw a lot of Skins wearing the German Army surplus shirt, the one with the little German flag on the arm. This wasn't a political statement; it just was a good Army Navy surplus shirt that was cheap and durable. I must say I didn't get one.

Now when it came to the wearing of the shoes, things have changed a bit for me now. When I was younger there was a tad gap between the top of the shoe and the hem of the trouser, either jeans sta-press or suit trousers. Well, I'm in my 50s now and it would look silly to have that gap, but I still wear red or white socks with the shoes; can't change everything.

Back to trousers: jeans, I must say Levis if possible, but even in the late 70s they were expensive, so Wranglers or any cheap pair of jeans would do, and also if you bleached them which was popular; an expensive pair of Levi's, unless old, you didn't bleach. Also Army surplus trousers were very popular. I used to like the black German moleskins. Many Skins wore these trousers, again cheap, and very long lasting. Well, we are working class and you bought what you could afford {unless a couple of your mates had done a little night time free shopping}. Sta-press were also still in vogue; they could be worn with shoes as well as your boots and they too came in various colours: white, black, blue, burgundy. I did like my burgundy and black pairs. I still do; at least you could wear them more than once. My missus hated the white; you only had to sit on a bus and they needed washing.

Jackets and coats: the Crombie was still worn and black, blue, grey and brown were most common. I did see a burgundy one that didn't look too bad – even better if you got velvet collar and pockets – real smart. Not so many donkey jackets: very rarely seen. I can't remember seeing a Skin in one for years. Sheepskin is a must. It's just got to be worn. Harrington Jackets still are popular; many colours there to choose. Jean jackets you must have had to have one in your time. Also some of us would wear one of your old two-tone jackets with your jeans and boots. It made a change and looked pretty good.

Then the new MA1 flying jackets were getting popular. Green and black the colours were and cost about £30. Not like now — if you want an original you have to take out a mortgage.

Also a lot of Skins would wear DP {army jackets} you got from army surplus. I was lucky; when I left the armed forces I still had a lot of kit to use. Headwear: well Skins still have the flat cap. I wear one and love it, but Trilbies and the pork pie hat are worn by many. So a lot of the clothes were still as the originals wore, but with a little tweaking here and there.

The girls: well they had changed to what or how I remember the original Wrens; the now seen Skin girl hair cut was the norm, and more girls wore boots: DMs, although Brogues and Loafers were and still are seen on the girls. Jackets and coats the same as the boys, But the big difference for me with the girls is their two-tone jacket and skirt combo, with the Fishnets. I just cannot remember that look from the days of my big bro, but that look nowadays is a wow; the girls just look sexy, but mean in that combo. I also see more girls with braces — again something I cannot remember from the original days.

Also the debate with lamb chops, or the good old sideburns. I can remember back in my brother Bob's day that a lot of the Skins had them, two sorts: the ones that look like the old lamb chops {how they got their name} and the smaller version that grew straight down the cheeks, only if you could grow them though, and to think about it, it's all down to genetics from your Dad and, let's face it, all the Skins who had Dads that were original Teddy boys were bound to get good old sideburns. So it was a must if you could grow them. When it came round to the Skins of our period, '76 onwards, not many had them, or chose not to have them. Many of the older ones still did, the ones left over from the early 70s, but they were going and leaving the future to the new breed.

Many new Skins had by now the number one cut or even closer, so the sideburns didn't look right, in fact, a bit stupid. A number two or three and they looked good, only a few could get away with a number one and still look okay.

Like many I kept my hair at number one and at times shaved my head completely. It was how the mood took you, but the elder me, and my brother got me started, keeping the hair number one or two and the lamb chops were grown, as I keep it now. I suppose it's a badge of honour and years as a Skin, but you do get idiots who look at you and say that the spirit of '69 look is associated with commie Skins. Fucking crap! I have been Skin a long time and I love the history of it and try now to keep it as it was: clothes, hair, lamb chops, music and attitude. I HATE POLITICS. ALL POLITICIANS are CRIMINALS and ALL POLITICS is CRIMINAL.

Teens 1976

We had left London by 1973 and moved to Reading, Mum and Dad's families were from Reading so it wasn't much of a change for them; for us kids, I don't think we cared, a house was a house

My school years were a laugh, not the most intelligent in the world, but smart in the real world. The secondary school I went to had a large proportion of coloured lads, and many were my friends and, because I already had a knowledge of Ska, got on well with them because of the music. There wasn't a lot of animosity at the time between black and white and I didn't care who anybody was; the only thing that stands out at that early age was the series: ROOTS. After this came out, all the coloured lads and girls got a bit of an attitude – did get an attitude – not being funny, but things did begin to change. I didn't give a shit; whatever happened in the past was the past. Bloody hell! Even my grandparents who fought in WW2 now worked side by side with Germans and Italians. No one told me to hate them, or hold a grudge and plenty of my family had been killed during the war, but I came to realise in later life that racialism is not endemic to just white people and it has no boundaries. Every nationality on this planet can be a racialist, and racists and anti-racists use it for their own greed and power. That's why I hate every fucking politician on the planet; each part of the biggest multi-organised crime syndicate in the world.

Being 15 and 16 and a teenager in the 70s and knowing lots of old Skins, my brother Dan and I were going to disco's that played some Ska, skinhead reggae, and *Slade* and *Judge Dredd*, as well as having to listen to what was popular then: The popular disco stuff (fucking awful) or the super group progressive rock crap. The songs went on for years, *Genesis*, yes, all that stuff, fucking spaced-out hippies — didn't understand it, still don't; the Glam thing was okay, even good, *Slade* did a massive help for Glam, and their history with our cult will never be forgotten.

Also there was that plastic rock 'n roll rubbish from *Showaddywaddy* and other such bands. I know they were, or probably thought they were Teds, but the proper Teds hated them. I made the mistake of asking some one day; oh my God it gave me an insight on how they felt, "fucking plastic rip-off teds they have fuck all to do with us". Point taken; never ask again.

We knew a lot of folks who were into the (then new) Punk scene. I was being drawn towards this, so yeah, I was a Punk. Dan by now had had his metamorphosis and was a 100% 24 carat Skin. I, on the other hand, was safety pinned-up, bin bags, coloured hair, the lot and was lucky enough to have an Aunty (through marriage who was a stunner, ooh how I loved looking at those legs, and she knew it) who worked for the London Arts school and who got passes for gigs all over the London area in schools and colleges. I was lucky enough to see *The Pistols* in Watford at the age of 16, and had some good times seeing the bands. The early Punk stuff did really give you a feeling of change, but then the money men got involved and made stars out of them — ruined it.

I took some beatings as well. I remember being chased all over the underground by Teds and RockaBillies and also getting a kicking from the notorious Millwall football hooligans. That did hurt; funny thing was they were all Skins, Herberts or Bootboys. They pinched my creepers I had on. I remember one saying "Take those shoes — Dad was a Ted". But you had to take the beatings; that's what happens when you get involved in street cults. It's a laugh, it hurts, but you grow up quick, not like nowadays with all this knife and gun worshipping, drug-fuelled rap and gangster crap, but there you go, things changed for the worst.

18

Anyway that was a good time for a while, into the Punk thing '75 through '76 until '77 when I too had a metamorphosis with help from Dan's mates.

August 1977

Still into the Punk scene.

I remember it well as it was two months before going into the RAF Regiment and the month I finally went Skin. I was going to meet Dan in one of the cafés he and the Skins used, so I was hoping to just give him a wave and off we'd go. As I approached the café: Greggs it was called (it was a meeting place for the Reading Skins and not the Greggs of today's multi coffee-drinking conglomerate), there already was a bunch of Skins outside. Oh my God, I thought – loads of DMs, shaved heads, Crombies and Harringtons and the first time I saw the MA1 jacket that got popular during this time. Strange looks as I approached: a Punk on his own going to a skinhead meeting place. I was shitting bricks, just hoping there had not been any Punk beatings the night before. There wasn't too much aggro between Punks and Skins in Reading, but things happen.

Fortunately I knew a lad and he obviously told the others I was little Dan's brother. I looked in the window and saw Dan. He was sitting with the top lads and a skingirl (RH) was mothering him. She had his head, hugging him to her rather large breast, patting him on the head {lucky sod}. I tried waving but he didn't see. I then had to take a deep breath, open the door and say, "Dan you coming?" which he did with a cup of tea in hand.

"Strange looks there, mate, I had," I said to him.

"Yeah, they said you are letting the side down," he replied.

With that statement, it changed me. I didn't want to let my brother down and I'd become fed up with the Punk scene anyway – it was just not the thing for me any more. I loved the music, but I suppose in my subconscious mind I'd been around Skin for many years and I was going to get a haircut anyway when I joined up. So with that, on the Saturday I was in the barber's getting my number 1, already had a pair of boots, a Crombie that Bob gave me and a few shirts. Dan gave me a pair of braces, and I looked the business. Dan had a great smile on his face, "Yep, you'll do – introduce you to Brian, and the crew."

That night, Dan took me down to a pub called *The Captain's Cabin*, (another pub that is not there any more). This was a little place the Skins used; you had to go down a flight of stairs to get into the bar, really dark and dingy. As you came down the stairs the bar was on the right and there were small tables and chairs in front of it. It wasn't a very wide place but the room stretched back quite a bit and all the Skins used the tables and snug holes at the back and darkest part of the bar. There the ones too young to drink would be hidden from view and have their sneaky beer as long as they didn't get rowdy or stupid. The landlord knew, but a blind eye was turned. Didn't matter how old the customers were, compared to money: the root of all evil.

This night was supposed to go just as a first meeting, an introduction to Dan's friends, and to show the crew a new member (me) and hope I would fit in. Dan was popular; he was only 5 foot 5, stocky, but he showed no fear and the elder Skins liked him for that, {unfortunately his actions and lack of fear were caused by an incurable brain disease we have in the family} and the fact the younger ones were always useful for the odd job of getting stuff, or doing stuff. It's life really – start at the bottom, work yourself up.

As well as blokes there were the girls; WRENS that's what they were called, and I got to meet my first lot of birds. Some were pretty; instantly thought, Oh God, yum yum, but there were a couple that looked like they fell out of the ugly tree. One girl in particular (JD), she had her hair cropped like the men and she was fairly broad. She had been just let out of a detention centre and she could fight; not clever in any way, but she was nice, as in do anything for her friends, and some used that. But she was a dirty cow, "Who wants to go in the bogs then?" That was one of her sayings. You all just looked at each other and hoped she didn't ask you, but I did like her; she made me laugh. It's a shame in later life that drugs ruined her.

As I remember, the night was going fine for my first introduction to the skinhead social scene. About eleven of us were in there: eight lads and three girls. Dan and I were the youngest there.

At the bar was a group of lads, six of them. Later to find out they were squaddies {soldiers} out for the night. Then all of a sudden all hell let loose, or so I gathered. Brian was at the bar with two other lads and one of the Wrens, JD. One of the lads, Bob (who wherever we went you knew he was there as he would shout out at the bar, "I'll have a light and bitter!") had asked for his drink. The bottle of light ale which was put on the bar for him to add to his bitter went missing; one of the squaddies had picked it up. Don't know if it was deliberate or accidental, but JD had seen it and without hesitation she just shouted,

"You barstard!" and threw a punch at the bloke. This resulted in his mates turning round and one of them gave JD a punch on the chin. She went flying; then all we saw was Brian pick up a stool and crash straight into the closest two. At the same time Bob had punched the closest one to him and had turned to attack the others. Well Brian and Bob were outnumbered even if they had taken out a couple. Without hesitation, me and Dan just charged, which action made the others with us act straightaway. My first bar fight: it didn't last long as I ran straight for the closest and didn't see his mate wallop the side of my head and out...

When I came round I'd been taken outside, and was held up against a wall while I got my head back together. I'd been dragged away from the bar as the police were called and on the way, the six squaddies had been well and truly fucked, and the only two who had been hurt a lot were JD and me. She had a massive cut on her lips and I had a headache and a jaw that hurt for days, but our actions had impressed the two top boys. Brian and Bob were well chuffed; they knew then that Dan and I were not just there as hangers-on, that we would stick with the crew and take punishment. Problem was JD had made straight for me. Well we had both been thumped and to her it was a calling card. I looked at Dan for help but his mother protector had him cuddled to her breast again, "AAAH LITTLE DAN, YOU OKAY – COME HERE." Big smile on his face.

Luckily for me, JD and the other two girls had to get back to their flat with some of the lads. They had just moved in; JD after her release and she needed help with some stuff. Dan and I, Brian and Bob all headed for the bus, all going the same way and staying in the town. We would have all been nicked without hesitation, but as Brian left the bus he said, "Pleased to know you, Spike. See you two boys tomorrow shopping in London." And that ended my first night out as a skinhead and a bar fight. Mum wasn't pleased when we got in. It was the usual. "Oh no what you been up to? Brian (Dad), look at the state of Russell (my real name)." Dad just looked. "If the peelers come round here you're out with your older brother." Needless to say, they didn't come, but the future would bring many and more sore nights, and police cells.

Politics

If you ever meet a person who was a Skin from the late 70s and 80s and they say they never got into politics, I'm afraid to say they're lying to themselves. You could not help being drawn into far right or far left. Not because you were just patriotic. Left or Right are both patriotic, but a lot of things were changing all around and you followed what your mates and family were doing; you were young and – well you went along with the flow, but the biggest influence was the music scene.

Yes there were real extremists already there and already in bands, but as I found out, being patriotic brands you, and that influences your psyche as to how you react. Extremist parties used bands that were popular to the scene and exploited that fact, and when you're young you make decisions that are not truly thought through; you have to live with that herd mentality and follow; your mates take control.

Deceitful, clever and manipulative people used our aggression and love for what we believe for their own greed and power, and skinheads and some Punks were targeted for that. My love for this country, its people and its history were used; my education was used, my skill from the armed forces was used, and many got away with their hate by using us – me and you. We got nicked and hurt; they got rich. Who was the fool? Records and band merchandise made some people very wealthy under the pretence of being into politics and the music, left or right. It just got the cult into massive violent conflict, arrested and, in some cases, death.

I myself was involved by playing in a band, being used, conned and treated like a twat. Yes it was patriotic, yes even extreme {far right} and

24

most probably over the top, but let's face it, things had radically changed in this country in the 70s and 80s. We saw a massive influx of immigrants {which is forgotten from that period} and street names WERE BEING CHANGED and foreign religious buildings were being erected everywhere, and no one was listening to us except the extremists, so they had us hooked and knew how to escalate to their needs.

NEVER AGAIN. Yes the songs were extreme. Yes, I was involved with extremists. But when you learn from hard knocks and being stitched and see others using you, a lesson is learned, and when people who are supposed to be your friends turn their backs on you or talk behind your back, because you don't want to be involved with shitty politics and politicians and you have made new friends like yourself who have seen the true cause of politics and seem like-minded as yourself, WERE YOU REALLY A FRIEND?

The extremist parties and politicians have used the skinhead scene for far too long, because it brings together people who, let's say, are a little more aggressive than the run of the mill populace. The left and right have managed, through lies and stealth, to split the cult completely down the middle. Skins fighting Skins just because of a political dogma: STUPID, FUCKING STUPID! And you would find in their record collection some Ska or skinhead Reggae Blue Beat – whatever on both sides of the political divide. But someone tells them they have to fight each other. It's about time we took our cult back from the bastards that have tried to destroy and corrupt it, and send them to their own little corners of the planet to fight for themselves and each other, without using us. ALL POLITICS is CRIMINAL and ALL POLITICIANS are CRIMINALS. That's how it has made me feel about this country's political scene. No, not for me – I'm out for a good time, friends, and some good old dancing. No doubt this will upset many. I'm not a traitor. I'm not a coward. I'm a realist. Anyone who attacked what I love: this island, its history, and my family, I would die fighting, but not for a stupid flag-waving bunch of uni educated twats trying to be working class. But hey-ho, we have to live with it.

1978 Reading Festival

The thing about this and, thinking back to those festivals then, it was a ROCK festival and none of this Rap and Hip-Hop and Dubstep you get now at festivals. YEAH, ROCK FESTIVAL. REALLY? Instead of ramming down the throats of people who like musicians playing guitars, drums and singing their own music, instead of one finger on a PC keyboard and sampling everybody else's music, FUCK OFF AND GET YOUR OWN FESTIVALS!

Anyway I digress. We knew it was going to be a good festival because of all the Punk and new wave bands that were booked and, to top it all, *Sham* was going to be playing; yeah and all that went with them. That Friday night couldn't come quickly enough; there were loads of us going, but like always there was a but – A BIG BUT – hardly any of us had tickets for that day, or just the evening, and the rumour went round they were not going to let Skins in that night.

We were already wound up for the entertainment. I think the idea was to go in about 5ish, but not through the main gates or trying to get through the fences; the plan was to go over the other side of the river, nick a boat and come in from the back of the site. We knew the area and knew there would be a boat or boats we could nick.

Whoever had the idea I don't know, but what a fucking brilliant one it was. And it was done: we nicked this boat; I don't think any of us had any idea how to run it, but hey, lots of beer and excitement, you try anything. Some of the Skins who couldn't get on the boat we nicked got into this little rowing boat. Six Skins trying to keep their balance and row across the river, all drunk and no idea at all. How they got across

I'll never know. We, on the other hand, had got the boat untied and, after going back and forth for a while, got in the right direction. The thing is, with a boat, currents are no help, and the river tends to flow, and a boat load of Skins pissed-up don't know this, and it was a laugh trying to get the boat on the correct course, even with an engine, and then the smiles. We were on the way – Vikings eat your hearts out – festival-goers, eat your hearts out too.

CRASH! Yep, the other bank – it's the easiest way to stop a boat. We all jumped off and headed across the fields and tents to the festival. Now the fun begins. There were loads of Punks, Herberts and Skins from all over, just waiting for the moment *Sham* came on and some of the other new wave and Punk bands, but we had time for more beer and to watch a few bands. One thing I can remember well: the HAIRIES WERE EVERYWHERE. Still a festival for old hippies to turn up to, and not just for the Rockers. As we all got together and started off towards the middle, we knew at some point violence was gonna happen. Then the god of war must have smiled on us. As we were pushing through, there was a hippy circle, all off their trolleys and singing. We made a bee-line for the circle. As we came close, Dan grabbed a massive can of Jackpot lager from one of them.

He just looked. "HEY MAN, SURE HAVE A DRINK."

We did, gone ours. The one in the middle with a guitar was the one leading the singing and just started going on about loving us. "HEY MAN, I LOVE YOU ALL. WE LOVE YOU ALL."

SMASH! I don't know who it was: Bob, Billy, Gashy or Carter, I can't remember, but the guitar was taken and smashed over his head, splinters everywhere and, as he was being hit, he still was giving his love. Wallop, wallop, wallop, boots into the rest. Move on, lots more victims of that day.

I can't remember too much of the bands. *Jam* were crap that's for sure; the idol that is, and thinks he is, Paul Weller had thrown his toys out of the pram 'cause the sound wasn't up to scratch. Fuck me, mate, you were supposed to be a Punk band – no one else had moaned. Jimmy Pursy had calmed the crowd down with a rendition of *You Will Never Walk Alone*, probably the only thing he did that day that didn't involve a fight, but that was all this day was about.

I also remember we had all crewed up and were standing near a lot of Angels. Risky, I know, but Bob knew some of them. When this young Skin walked through to meet us, an Angel stuck an umbrella under his chin and it had a sharpened point. It looked a nasty moment, but Bob stepped in and the lad was pulled away. That could have been nasty and not just for that night, but even after that night all people can remember is the skinhead violence, and nobody mentions that day and night the Angels were also smacking and cracking heads; it just didn't have the two cults fighting that day, thank fuck. I'm going to admit that day and evening is a long time ago and some things I'm telling probably happened in no specific order; it's just my own impression again.

Now the moment we had been waiting for: *SHAM* came on. We had all got to the front and already gone mad, the hairies were already walking out with bloody noses and tensions were high. The band came on and into their set and, as the norm, a load of pissed-up Skins started fighting. I'll admit anything that was not looking Punky or Skin was thumped and kicked. Pursey tried his best to calm the violence, but the Monster had been made and it was out of the lab and causing havoc, no matter what he said. Then, I don't know who and I think it was playing *Borstal Break Out* {could be wrong} a can came over and smashed into the bassist. The music stopped; we went mad, steamed the stage, hit everybody just to get there and, from that moment on, it was Armageddon. Too drunk to care, too excited to stop and who the fuck was gonna stop us anyway?

No matter how many tears Pursey had that day and how much John Peel asked for calm it was never gonna happen –it was fate and, even if you were not a *Sham* Skin, you just got into the fighting and, as I said before, the last time I saw them was as a Punk in their early days, and had been on the receiving end of *Sham* Bootboys, Skins and Herberts. Now I was in the front, at the point of causing it. How life changes.

After the *Sham* debarkle had finished, Dan and I, now very drunk and having had a night full of violence, decided to go home. A few of us had decided enough is enough and at some point one of us was going to get nicked. Well we did, but outside. As we left the site, a stupid fucking hippy and his mates, too stoned to realise who they were approaching, asked us if we wanted some blow. We just looked at each other and wallop! We kicked the shite out of them and, as we were dragging one off to do more violence, whom we said we were going to hang, coppers steamed us. They didn't care that they'd been going to sell drugs, and offered them to us – it was 'nick the skinheads for violence'. Dan, me, and Bristol Dave all got nicked and on the Tuesday the twenty-five pound fine for fighting was put up to fifty quid and a year's probation, which for me and Dan would end in tears when we got back to camp {being still in the services}.

We got a month in Innsworth {an armed forces prison}. But, hey, you do the crime, do the time. We both did it with a smile of resignation.

30

1979 Festival

Well, could it be as good? Unfortunately a big NO. The Friday night was the Punky night and it had *The Cure* who I'd seen that year earlier in Stafford, a strange band, couldn't work them out. *Motorhead* was to play and they were a noisy band. Punks, Hairies, Angels and some Skins liked listening to them – they were just so noisy. I also remember *The Tourist* playing. I haven't got a clue why. I'd seen them earlier in the year, I think with *Undertones* in Birmingham. They were okay for an inside gig, new wave at best, but for an outside Festival, bad choice, and I think they flopped. I think I even threw cans at them that night; there was a can fight between Punks and Rockers; we had to join in there, but nothing like the year before. I personally think the people who ran the festival then lost their bottle and a big chance for a great Punk festival.

The Banshees, *Clash* and even *The Pistols* could have and should have been booked, but they lost the chance. Instead to top the Bill that night they had *The Police*. I honestly didn't think that would go down well, but hold my hands up, they did recapture a festival feeling. In fact, although I don't like them, they were a good sound. But we didn't steam the festival like the year before; we didn't do a Viking raid. In fact, I think all the boats had been told to move. We had the odd punch-up but the Bill were on to us and watching all the time, and not so many had gone.

I lost Dan that night; he went off with this hippie chick and stayed in a tent with her for two days, and they were not talking about the state of the planet. He always said that was the best dirty weekend he'd ever had, so this festival wasn't that good, except I walked away with this massive back pack – huge it was. I just picked it up on the way out. That's heavy, I thought. Bloody full of beer: result.

1979 Shopping

Just a normal day in Reading town centre. We had met up about 11ish round the station: about eight of us, three Wrens, five blokes, nothing really important to do, just hang around different parts of the town and have a chat and a laugh, terrify the locals, maybe go into the local Chelsea café for tea, milk and a pasty. Dan was in prison, so he wasn't with us; he had gotten two years. After a short time of deciding what to do, it was "let's go have a couple of pints". Always a good idea and at the pub we could chalk up on the slate a couple of beers. About six o'clock we decided to just go into the town for a walk; we didn't get too far, stopped and all sat down on some steps that were an exit for a Sainsbury's shopping store, all closed up and lights off. We weren't gonna get told to move on or have the Bill come to move us on; we were just laughing about and chatting. One of the Wrens {Nikki, I think} just leaned against the shop double door. IT OPENED. We all looked at each other and smiled.

Blakey said, "Just give it a push — is it open really?"

Nik pushed again. Yep, it opened. Excitement and smiles instantly on all our faces. "Is anyone in the shop?" someone thought to ask.

"Don't look like it — they fucking forgot to lock up." That was it; we were in; already a bit tipsy because of the beers in the pub, and like a bunch of kids finding a chocolate box, we just stood around the shop floor, open-mouthed, wondering what to do first. It was one of those moments when stupid things happen. Blakey took off his loafers and put his socks on his hands; we just creased up. "What — I'm not leaving any prints?"

That's not what just creased us all up; he grabbed a shopping trolley and proceeded to do his weekly shop, up and down the aisles. The rest of us just went for the aisle where the booze was – had to be done. I grabbed a basket and loaded it with vodka, whisky and rum, "Fuck it, need beer," I was saying out loud to myself, bumping into the others who were looking for their favourite tipple, baskets in hand. Then I saw Squid, I think, pushing a trolley loaded with drinks.

"What the fuck are you going to do with that lot ?" I said.

"Yer, think about it Squid – how you gonna get that lot down the steps and not get noticed?" one of the girls said. He just smiled, shrugged his shoulders and moved on.

While all this was going on in a completely dark store, all we could hear was Blakey. "Anyone seen the tomato soup or Weetabix?" Again we just creased up; the excitement of what we were doing was making us all laugh, but Blakey walking round the shop barefoot {he left his loafers outside – why he didn't put them on with no socks who knows?} with socks on his hands, doing his shopping and muttering to himself just topped off the funny moment; he was a natural comedian and I don't know if he was just playing at what was happening or natural, and to top it he had this lazy eye that just wandered, you just creased up when you looked at him. We were robbing; he was shopping – it just had to be seen.

Needless to say, after what seemed an hour but was probably twenty minutes, we were all outside; we even helped Squid with his trolley full of bottles and cans. He was going to push his trolley to the room he rented which was not too far. He got nicked pushing his trolley later on. Blakey had by now his shopping in bags and was gonna go home, but first a little tipple from what we all got. What to do now, we all thought. PUB; no questions asked. We will be let in to lie low for a while – a few bottles given to the landlord and to cover our tabs. He won't mind; money wasn't it. I don't know how, but we must have been seen as the plod came in haste. I, by now, had gotten to the bus stop and, with my few bottles, was on my way home. Unfortunately for the others, six of the eight were nicked and, as sadly as always, fingers were pointed at people for grassing. I don't know who did or if they did, but mud sticks, and later in life many people have told me who grassed. I'm not going to mention their names; I didn't get nicked. I don't know if they did, or like in life, people fall out with each other and make up stories. All I can say is it was a fucking funny half hour and Blakey and his trolley and wonky eye will always stay in my mind.

1979 Elephant Man

I was on leave, came home and organized to meet all on the Saturday morning. It was also going to be a big football derby game. I'm not sure who Reading had but I know it was a derby: a local rival (just can't remember who it was). We were all going to meet up and trot off to football, hopefully keeping an eye out for the opponents, then ambush and lay into them. Dan and I got into town about 9:30am and we walked round until we met some others. Not many in town yet, as it was early. We then met Dave J, Taff, Chaff (who later became a scummy crackhead) and two others: can't remember their names.

Also my sister was there: Tania; it was her first invite to come along and meet the crew or crews. Mum had given us the orders: "Look after her; don't get into any trouble." Ooops, sorry Mum, but it wasn't our fault. We were outside a shop, *Quicksilver*, I think, when we heard a noise coming from just around the corner; the next thing we saw was a film crew walking backwards and filming up the road. Then we saw what they were filming: from around the corner came a firm of Skins, about thirty of them, stoked up by the film crew no doubt, and all pissed-up already, and angry. There was nowhere to go; they made a bee-line for us.

As they came across the road, they shouted, "Get the Reading hardboys!" The two that ran I can't remember; they lost their bottle and just ran (thanks). I pushed my sister into the *Quicksilver* shop and told her to stay; then they were on us. In this situation it is just a mess; it's fight for your life. I had two steam into me and push me against a wall; at the same time I saw a mob attack Dan, Taff and Dave. They were pushed back towards an alley, trying to protect themselves. That's when I lost sight of them. Meanwhile these two who attacked me had a surprise. I went crazy ape shit, decked one and pushed the other away. Oh dear, as I did this there were loads waiting to tear me to pieces. All I saw was this Skin come at me with something in his hands; it was a hammer – crack in the side of the head, stars and ringing behind my eyes, but to his and my surprise I didn't go down. It must have been some sort of self preservation instinct, but I just grabbed him and lifted him up, charging towards the *Quicksilver* window: CRASSSSSSSSSH! I put him straight through the glass.

With all this going on, the shoppers already in town were screaming and running away, and as the window went in there was just complete mayhem and more screams. I turned round ready for the complete slaughter I was about to get, catching out of the side of my eye the fucking film crew filming the whole lot – bastards! Just as I was expecting the end, a massive black guy came out of the pack of Skins; I don't know if he was a Skin or just a hooligan that came along. My head hurt and was ringing; I had been kicked and punched and I hurt all over and was seeing stars as well. He held out both arms and said, "STOP. THIS GUY IS OKAY; HE STOOD HIS GROUND."

Thank fuck for him. I'd have been kicked all over the place. As I staggered towards the unbroken shop window for support, my sister came out and pulled me in. All I saw was the mob staring at me, swearing and moving on to meet some other poor soul to be twatted, while picking up the Skin who went through the window; his head was pissing blood. But then out of the corner of my eye, I saw Chaff; he was hiding behind some shop advertisement so no one could see him. He had left me to get a kicking. As they all walked off my sis took me by the arm to lead me out of the shop. "Let's find Danny, Russ. Are you okay?"

"I hurt, but first I want to talk to him," pointing to Chaff.

I walked over to him; he just looked at me and said, "They must've thought I was with them."

"You fucking hid mate. Don't make up stories – you hid. My sis saw you and even she tried to have a go."

I just shook my head and Tania and I went looking for the others. I saw what way they went and headed for the alley. As we went into it there were shoppers everywhere, on their arses or swearing; they obviously had gotten in the way of the battle of the alleyway. Just innocents but, hey – in that scenario you either move or get hurt. As we walked down the alley, Dan and the others came out of a shop.

"Fuck me. What happened to your head?" Dan said.

"Fucking hell, Spike. Is your eye in there? Your side of your head and eye are huge!" Dave added.

That seemed to bring me around a bit, the pain began to take effect, and I saw myself in the shop window. I looked like the Elephant man – a complete mess. We decided to go the long way round town and head for a pub called *The Star*. We knew some footy lads met there and the word could get out about what just happened. Also we had to get off the street as the Bill were looking to arrest all.

Well for me and Dan the day's events were at an end. It was too dodgy to take Tania around town knowing there were firms about after trouble; plus we all had had a kicking, and I was a mess, and I knew when I got home Mum was going to go mad, but I couldn't forget the fact that Chaff had let us and himself down. It got about quite quickly, and he soon grew his hair and left the skinhead scene. I saw him about two years after this on a bus. He looked a mess: long greasy hair, out of his head. He just looked at me while on the bus and said in a spaced-out hippy way, "Oh yeah, Spike ent it? Uhhhh, something to do with Dan."

Fucking hippy c**t! I just smacked him in the head and gave him a couple of punches. Fucking arsehole – you earnt that. I don't forget.

Millwall Gets Me Again

I've said in a previous chapter about when I was a Punk and Millwall fans gave me a slap and pinched my shoes. Well, talking again to my sis, she reminded me of one time outside the barber's.

Every two weeks we used to go down town to a barber's shop just on the Oxford road called Alfonso's. Yep, he was an Italian and a bloody good old bloke and barber (he even gave my bro and I a lift one day when we were returning back to camp from leave, just pulled up and said, "Get in lads, I'll take you.") plus, he had two stunning daughters.

There we would all sit outside and inside waiting for our turn to have the barnet cut. With the Skins that day was our usual gang of Punks which were part of the tight mob Dan and I went around with. I think Andy Benham (another one of those Punks with an impish grin, but a great bloke, 100% 24 carat Punk) was there, also. With him, was Shaun Doyle, as were some more Punks, but these two stood out, probably because they were just good mates. Also there were some girls: Skin girls and those that hung around with us who had not yet taken the plunge and the metamorphosis to be Skin, my sis being one of them.

Typical Saturday morning; we were having or just about to have the hair cut, sitting around outside. Then from nowhere, and I cannot even remember them walking up the road, a gang of blokes, not just young youths, came from over the road and from around the corner, then just laid straight into us, no hanging about. They knew what they were about to do; our unfortunate day was to have just met the famous Millwall football bushwhacker hooligans.

We knew it was a footy day and it was Millwall, but didn't expect them to be this far from the ground and this early. I was hit and kicked about a bit, but some of us, including Tomo, a Skin who was a Millwall fan, were seriously laid into.

I know Malcolm was given a good hiding and then thrown over a hedge and he hit a wall and fell down a front cellar. He wasn't well after that. I also think (sorry, mate, if it wasn't you, but sis thinks it was) Wayne had a serious kicking.

Everybody else, and it wasn't fear but self preservation, did a tactical withdrawal to anywhere safe. My bro and some of the others were locked in the barber's when the trouble started. The shop didn't want anyone coming in, and no-one could hold it against them.

This was an attack from a serious professional bunch and grown *big* men most of them. Maybe one on one you could have held your ground for a while, but this lot, you had to give them loads of respect just because they were so good. I learned a lesson: get in fast, get it done and get away... RESPECT, MILLWALL.

Crass, Reading Town Hall 1980/81

Crass was coming to Reading – yippee! This would be fun. Everybody knew about *Crass* and the bands that followed them on tour; no matter what we thought of their politics, a few of us had their records, but it was the thought of all those anarchist Punks and hippies that followed them. Yep, we were going to the concert for one reason: WAR. For all their anarchist beliefs, *Crass* were pretty good at making plans and organisation. The tour was out there to see where they were going to play and the bands that would be with them. That was pretty damn good for anarchism, but hey, the more organised their tour, the more they would bring and the bigger the rumpus would be.

The day of the concert was pretty low key for us in the town centre; we met up, went down the local we used then {Britannia} and talked about the coming fun. It would be a good turn-out: Skins, Punks and the girls would all be there from our crews, and we all knew at sometime during the night the fun would start. Dan and I left to go to the pub about 6ish, after an afternoon of special boot polishing. Mum gave us the speech before going out, "NO FIGHTING, NO POLICE". Oops, sorry Mum, but the night's entertainment just happens to have more than music involved.

We were in the pub about 6:30 {early start} and halfway through the first drink by 6:33. Dan and Rich T {who sadly is not with us any more} were at their usual best of taking the piss out of this Punk girl who came into the pub. Her brother was a Skin and they were from an Italian family; they were both nice people, but she had a bit of a big nose. She wasn't ugly, but Dan and Rich, every time she came in, made a point of taking the piss covertly. Back then in the 80s Guinness used to have a toucan as a brand logo – a big picture on the bar. When she came in, they would pinch the picture, go sit by her and put the picture of the toucan next to her. They would then,when she would be looking at one with her back to the other, make gestures with their hands about how big her nose was and point to the toucan's beak. She never caught on, but I and others would be in fits, pissing ourselves, while Dan and Rich T would be acting all lovely and normal – it was a great double act.

So another good night in the Britannia; we did have a few. Many a mess I would leave in that place. The drink we had then was what we called the green bottle; it was the original Heineken bottles; little ones they were. Dan and I would go into the pub and buy a complete case of twenty-four; that would last and your mates could have some too.

We left for the gig about 8pm; only a short walk through town to the old town hall, where the gig was on. As we came up to the hall we met more of the local Skins and Punks, a good crew of about 100 of us, but take out the wannabes and the girls, we would number about fifty strong, enough for a laugh. We went in: the usual search; oh joy they had their own *Crass* security, not local firms from town or the council, and – guess what – they were arrogant.

Strike one: we'd had a beer and arrogant anarchist security. An argument started at the door; they weren't going to let in one of our girls. I can't even remember why, but the tension started then. "You don't let her in, mate, it's going off now and there won't be a gig – the Bill will close it down." The thought crossed the dozy-looking hippy twat and she was let in. It was packed; there were Punks and hippy anarchists from all over the country, and when we walked in it was like a western: quiet and stares. The Punks that were with us made their way over to where the other local Punks were: a good crew, always good reserve if things got dodgy. Us lot walked over to the side of the stage; that was going to be our base of operation. Then the bad news; this time Rich Q and Dan, Rich T and Ronni came over from where the bar was. "They're charging 2 quid a can of fucking beer." {it was in the 80s} "I'm not paying that price for the shit they're selling." Hoffmeister, I think Dan said. So Beer was out.

Strike two: so the next idea was to go to the exit stairs and send one of the young ones or girls to get some plonk from the take-out; the usual brought back for the time Merrydown cider, some Courage lagers and the ruin of many: vodka. Strangely, the shitty security didn't stop us drinking it by the door. Oh what a mistake to make; while the first bands were on, *Poison Girls*, I think, we were getting wrecked, and more agitated with the amount of anarchists and hippies about. At about 10ish *Crass* came on. We made our way back to the side of the stage, transfixed by a massive screen behind the band showing videos of war and nasty things from history, as they played. This just made us more excited. Halfway through the gig a video came on; it was 1930s Germany. Nuremberg and German troops marching; good, bad, let's face it, it was part of the cult. We got dragged into it – you didn't have to be a fully fledged Nazi or Fascist; these videos just did things to you, and the booze helped.

Grainger jumped up on the stage; he did some form of silly dance and the usual right arm salute to Steve Ignorant {the singer}. I'd also climbed onto the stage followed by Dan and I think Rich Q, and some others. By this time the band's security had also come onto the stage – one of them was massive. They grabbed Grainger.

Strike three: he took this as an attack; Grainger threw the first punch. I'd seen this and, as the other security came to stomp Grainger, I'd arrived and charged the hippy who had grabbed him first around the waist. As I brought my body and head up, the massive ugly fuck had also tried to engage – CRACK – the top of my crust caught his chin. FLOP – he hit the floor, just at the right time. As he hit the floor Dan and the others had arrived – right – boot – smack as he hit the floor {the ugly massive fuck}. Dan's boot hit his head. Rich and the others had now rescued Grainger and all hell was let loose, as more of the band's security came out and entourage. We just attacked, and as I looked down to where all the others were standing, security were trying to stop more getting onto the stage, and there was war going on there. As usual a big space had opened up around where the trouble was. This had brought the more heroic hippy to have his say, or try to put in the odd 'boot and run' tactic, but those by the stage were having tremendous fun dropping bodies everywhere, and by now the Reading Punks, who usually hung around with us, also decided to join in and have a bash at the anarchist Punks and hippies. Oh the joy! This all happened in seconds, but looking from the stage it seemed like an hour – the excitement, beer and joy had just got to me. Bang! side of the head – that will teach me – dreaming again – a bottle from somewhere, but it brought me back to reality. Dan, Rich and Grainger were by now holding their own and going at anyone with anything that came towards them. Now it was time to take on the band as well, as more of the Reading Punks and Skins got onto the stage. We made a direct attack on the band – no reason, they were just there and had a lot of mouth, and the alcohol-fuelled adrenalin attack reached its climax inside the hall. The band got off stage quick; what was left of the security also made a retreat. That was the cue for tactical withdrawal; the Bill would be here as soon as we all made for the door. The gig was over; whoever wasn't involved had already run for the exit or hid themselves for their own protection. Our enemy for the night had thought about the situation and decided we were too nasty – no, just fuelled up for the night's entertainment and a laugh.

As we moved outside, the local plod had arrived in force. Some of the lucky ones had made the street outside, but about twenty of us were still trying to get out when the plod steamed in. It didn't matter who they hit to get to us and bodies flew everywhere, but they came to get us, just to arrest us. We had nowhere to run to, night sticks coming down at us and we just had to protect the head, dogs barking and chomping at the bit to bite, we were dragged outside, not even put up against the wall, made to lie on the floor, bleeding from the plod attack not the fight inside. Okay, I thought, did my brother get out? Where is he? Then I heard his voice, "SPIKE YOU OKAY?"

"YER MATE, YOU?" I said.

"NO, SOME FUCKING COPPER HAS NICKED MY ZIPPO!"

Of all the things that night, Dan thinks about his Zippo lighter. Mum and Dad will go ape when they find out we are nicked, I thought, but to all our astonishment the plod made us all stand up, no charges? There was no video evidence {very rare back then} and *Crass* did not press charges. Fair play to them; they stood by that rule of anarchism. No police; {but no doubt the local press and music press would slag us down, but warranted this night} don't trust the police, and because none of the innocents who had got hurt were outside yet, still afraid to come out in case of more trouble or getting nicked, no one was pointing fingers at any of us. The only one to get nicked was one of the young Wrens, as she had all the booze in a bag and was a tad tipsy and too young to drink and be in possession of alcohol. So the night had ended okay for us – well mostly, battered and bruised, but laughing our heads off, talking about the night's entertainment: what we did, what we said. It's always the same after the fight: the big talk yourself up, but then the thought, FUCK IT – NO BUSES – GOT TO WALK HOME.

Rich Q and me

The Party

Parties back in the late 70s through the 80s were everywhere, and you had to go. Also, if there was a rich bird (there were loads), who tagged onto a Punk or Skin, these parties were the tops. Fun was to be had and just our luck, Graham, a Punk and great mate, had such a bird and a party was had. Oh how she must have wished she never had met Graham and his mates: US. We all met up in the local boozer for the end of the week piss-up. A hard week working; now Friday night to get wasted.

Dan and I got into the pub at about 7pm; there we met other mates, Skins and Punks, and there started our weekend of refuelling. Then Graham came in with his new girlfriend, as always a nice looking bird; cannot remember her name, but a punky looking girl.

As we were having our beer, Graham told Dan and me he was going to a party at his girlfriend's friend's house: a birthday party it was and she had said he could invite Dan and me. Fantastic, we thought, let's not get too pissed here, save some money and go for it at the party. Then Graham tells us where it is: one of the posh parts of town. Result: the night just got better and maybe some more rich fillies would be there.

As always, after a few beers, Graham had talked his girlfriend into letting some more come. Well that meant open house to us lot, and so we all trotted off to the party: a good group of Skins and Punks, all looking forward to having a laugh.

When we got to Woodley (the posh part), things had changed. All the houses were huge, long driveways, big gardens and posh cars. I know it's bad, but all we thought about walking through this part of Reading was what we could take. We wouldn't have done it, but it was the thought (luckily Waistcoat and Gav were not there; they would have stripped the places), and looking at this lot, they wouldn't have even missed it. How the other side of society lives; never had to go without dinners or heating, or even had the cops turn up at their houses. I suppose it's the same for the rich and wealthy everywhere.

Anyway, we got to the house. Just as we thought, full of rich kids dressing like Punk and Goth to shock their Mums and Dads. Posers, I suppose. Okay to stand about in the local shopping area or street corner or park, but not the real deal to hang around town with all the 100%ers; but I must say it was full of fillies, nice ones.

They all seemed fine when the Punks with Graham and his girlfriend walked in, but when us lot followed the faces changed a tad. A case of, oh dear, what are *they* doing here?

As was the norm, the first thing we aimed for was the fridge and the beer. We asked where the kitchen was and made a beeline for it. No one stood in our way and a picture of joy came to our faces as we entered the kitchen: beer and alcohol everywhere. It was Skinhead drinking heaven. To our amazement, more than one room had had a fridge put there for beer. Yum, yum, we wouldn't have to worry as long as they were kept stocked up.

Second on the list was to take over the music, head for the stereo and find some tunes to get the party going from mellow to shock. We put some of our girls near the stereo to make sure it didn't get silly. I know it wasn't our party, but there was always someone at these birthday bashes that wanted to play some of the popular disco crap that was in the charts NOOOOOOOOOOOO; it's bad enough having to watch the crap that was on *Top of the Pops* every Thursday night, or *Radio One* — painful to say the least.

Well the party went well; we were getting drunk and messing about, taking the piss and having a laugh. Even Graham joined us; the beer was taking effect. It was getting late; parents were not coming back and we were going into silly mode, as you do at parties. When the beer has taken you over, you go on the house investigation, follow the girls around and check out all the rooms, especially the ones upstairs. Fabulous — not only loads of rooms but a fecking great big fridge upstairs and, with the lateness of the night and the alcohol, we got hungry and this fridge was full of food. Dan, me, Shorn the Punk, Graham and Beaker raided the fridge. It was like a swarm of locusts; just open the fridge and put as much food in the mouth as you can, all the while laughing our heads off.

Then it happened: one of the posh Punks at the party asked us, "DO YOU MIND NOT DOING THAT? IT'S SOMEONE'S FOOD."

What a mistake to make: a posh punk, asking four pissed-up Skins and two Punks to mind what they were doing. Dan just looked at him and threw some food at his face. We just creased up, and the posh Punk looked like he was going to cry. Too late to stop now; we had started. Beaker then grabbed what I think was potato salad; he put it straight over the posh Punk's head, followed by a FUCK OFF! from us all. The bloke then turned away and went back to his friends.

By now, it wasn't just us who were getting out of order. The front door was open and a few of the other Punks and Skins were rolling about outside in the flowers, trying to be stopped by a brave friend of the birthday girl, but again a tirade of abuse being aimed at him. He turned away, I think by now heading for Graham's girlfriend to ask for help. Also the girls had started as well. They were now arguing with anybody at the stereo who just didn't look like they were enjoying what they had decided to play. It was getting to go mental time for us.

Looking back, I know it was wrong, but when you're young, drunk and having a laugh with mates, you just can't stop yourself.

By now the beer had really taken effect, the fridge was empty and so we had the idea of taking it out of the room and standing it on the landing. Graham, Shorn, Beaker and I dragged it out to the landing, being watched by all the other party-goers. Some of them were actually laughing; alcohol had got to them as well, but their smiles wouldn't last.

Dan, by now, had gone outside for a piss, and missed the fridge-napping and, as we were thinking what to do with the thing, we heard a noise. Dan came straight through the front door on a moped, beeping the horn and laughing his head off. We were again in stitches and egging him on. He then decided to go up the stairs on the bike — bodies just jumped out of the way as he zoomed to the top of the stairs. By now all hell had gone off in the house. The girls were laying into anyone who confronted them, and all of us who had turned up at the party were in rooms all over the house, emptying the fridges and causing mayhem. Graham's girlfriend and her sister were going mad. We *had* to leave. Oh yeah? Not yet. Dan had now decided to ride the moped up and down the landing of the stairs, in and out of rooms, and terrifying anyone in the way. We now decided to see if a fridge bounced; we picked it up and threw it over the stairs — SMASH! It didn't bounce, but made a massive noise and mess, with people diving out of the way.

Dan now zoomed back down the stairs, the bike bouncing all over the place like he was riding a buckarooing mule. He went straight outside and rode round the garden. Us lot were now being chucked out of the house. We could have totally gone mental and handed out some good hidings, but we were all drunk and laughing too much and we all knew what was coming next. Yep, the old Bill would probably nab a few of us, so we all decided to get back to town — too late for a bus; no taxi would pick us lot up, and we probably didn't have enough money.

We now waited for Dan to stop playing on the moped, and just for his entertainment he headed straight for the pond — a big pond, and just before he and the bike went flying into the murky water, he jumped off and we all watched the bike go splash and sink to the bottom of the small lake they called a pond. Well that night's entertainment was over; it was a long trek home and, by luck or divine intervention, we didn't get nicked.

Now let's get something straight: not all the parties we went to ended up in mayhem; most were just a laugh and nothing happened, except we got drunk, loads of Wrens and fun was had. Yep, now and again a fight was had, but we were Skins and violence went with it, same as having a laugh. Things have changed now. I'm an old man, an old Skin, and I think my maturity has finally made me see that the ways of old were a tad OTT. But there you go — we were young and irresponsible, probably like most young peeps, when fuelled by drink, even nowadays.

A Bad Gig Night

During my time in the RAF, I was stationed in Stafford. Most of my friends were in civvies, Skins and Punks, so much of my off-duty time was spent with them, although, when Dan and I got stationed there together, we got our own firm within the RAF: Punks and Skins. That didn't go down well at all. Anyway, we found out that *Cockney Rejects* were to play in Birmingham, and we ended up at the Cedar club, which will go down in musical riot history. I, Bounce, and two civvy Punks from Stafford decided we would go. It was just a Punk gig, although Bounce and I knew that the band had had some trouble with NF and BM skins, which had resulted in fights because the Far Right was not tolerated at the *Rejects*' gigs. Again, the extremist left and right wanted to be aligned to them, but no one could get it into their heads that this lot had their own politics. It was called West Ham, and they were proud of that fact, and probably the love for that football club is what ended their potential fame. It didn't help having Trotsky Bushell tagging along; his mouth got the band into trouble and he didn't help them, either. He couldn't get it into his head that the *Cockney Rejects* and West Ham were one and the same: no politics, just West Ham.

Anyway, off we went to the gig. I was the only one a bit anxious, as my accent is a Berkshire one and in Birmingham I got funny looks all the time. Bounce was a Geordie and the other two had the local Potteries accent, and sometimes I was called a Londoner, for some reason. Well, I suppose if you don't live down south you don't recognise the difference. Bounce was the typical Skin from up north; he had a big love for Northern soul, as well, and had the odd Northern soul patch on his MA1 jacket, and a patch with Wigan Casino – if you knew Northern soul, you knew that place. A lot of Skins up north danced to that, in with Punk Ska and the two-tone stuff.

We got to Birmingham round about 6ish and made for a bar that the two lads from Stafford knew about (opening times were different back then; pubs actually closed for a time). So, after a couple of pints, Bounce and I followed the two mates to the club. I can always remember the street, Constitution street or road, and the club was on a corner. When we arrived, there was a queue and we joined, waiting for our turn to be searched to go in. There were Punks there, and herberts and, luckily, a few Skins – local boys, but at least other Skins had turned out. I also noticed a lot of smoovies, going to a punk gig, which was strange? They all looked like the local footie hoolies.

I could not believe the place when we got in: a tiny stage in the middle of the floor and the place was bigger than it looked from outside. Yeah, a typical Punk do, like back in the era 75, 76, 77. I'd been to a lot of gigs like that. I also noticed some lads had come up from London to see the band; they must have been friends, as well as fans of the band, and by the look of them they were not a bunch of pussies – about twenty of them in Brummy – respect, and they were all bunched together, minding their own business.

We got our place to wait for the band and we saw a few Punks and Skins from Stafford and the surrounding areas, so at least we knew some other bods there and every now and then, when I spoke, I had some strange looks, the accent was being noticed. Thank fuck I had the two from Stafford and others (who knew me) around and Bounce and his "can't understand a word he says" Geordie accent. I was just having a swig of my beer, chatting to Bounce, when some of the smoovies came up. They looked at me and Bounce and said, "Where you from?"

We looked at each other and I said, "Stafford."

"You're a Cockney," one of them said.

"No, he isn't, he's a yokel farmer, from Berkshire, Reading," Bounce said. Well, I think he said that; you couldn't tell half the time.

The gang who by now had moved near to us just looked at each other. Bounce had totally confused them with his accent and I don't think they knew where Berkshire was. Just as I thought things were going bad, they noticed the two Punks with us, (sorry I can't remember their names now). Thank fuck one of them used to be a Punk and recognised our mate. They asked them if we were with them and they said yeah, we live in Stafford. They didn't tell them we were servicemen; I think that would have just been the end – two out of town skinheads – one with a dodgy southern accent and in the forces. We would both have had the shit kicked out of us then. Anyway, things seemed to calm down and they moved off, so we decided we would move further into the hall, near the far wall. We could then see what was going on and nobody could smack us in the back of the head.

This was not going to be good, I thought; these blokes were not Punks or herberts and they were going round recruiting more to their numbers (Punks and herberts) all the time. I think the boys from London knew this, but it was a gig; you always had a sense of something going on. That's what made Punk gigs fun and exciting, but this night had a bad feeling. I really was concerned; it felt like a bad football terrace scenario. Then I noticed a couple of them had on football tops: Birmingham City. Oh no, the penny dropped, this lot were footie hoolies and had come to the gig for nothing more than to have a dig at the *Rejects* and their followers, all because they were West Ham. I hoped this would just be a lot of banter and that was all.

I can't remember when and how the fight started. Yep, the banter was strong, the band had come on and the shit had started straight away – typical football type chanting and hostility. I don't think the band had time to plug in; then, all of a sudden, mayhem. The City boys started having a go at the boys from London and the band, glasses, chairs, all sorts of things were being thrown. As well as the charge and attack, the boys from London had nowhere to go but fight, to fend off the firm that now tried to get the upper hand, and numbers count, no matter how hard you are. Even the band was fighting – this lot from London was not going down without taking some with them. Our two mates had the right idea: straightaway they made their way to the exit for safety, while we two were stuck halfway. The last thing I saw of the band was one of them being set upon and being smashed over the head with a glass or something. It didn't look good; also some of the London crew were getting the boot laid into them on the floor. Bounce and I knew at any time we were going to get dragged into this if we didn't make a way out. I'd been in concert fights before: *Sham*, *Upstarts* and others, but this was different. When these fights happen, they happen quick; it's in and out as fast as you can, do as much damage as you can, but nobody was trying to stop it. This just carried on; it was complete mayhem. The Plod would be called and then it'd be every man for himself. What we couldn't understand was where the bouncers were? We did see the band being moved to one side, but it just got worse – why didn't the bouncers help? Well, they did help. We both saw them laying into the London lot. This all had to be planned. It wasn't the usual spontaneous ruck; this poor lot were being assaulted from all sides, not one on one, twos and threes laying the boot in and punching, all because of football – that's all this was about, but those West Ham boys didn't run. As we got to the door some of the city boys were running out, job done – they had the numbers and did their damage. To them it was a victory. As one went past – bang! Bounce was smacked in the head; we were just nearing outside when this happened, and the force of the impact made Bounce stumble out into the street. I tried to follow as fast as I could. I knew if he wasn't out cold he would fight. Just as I saw him turn round – wallop! I saw a fist come round and smack me in the mouth; my front bottom tooth instantly came out and blood spurted everywhere. As I now stumbled to the street and spat the tooth out – crack! – another punch as someone ran past. Both Bounce and I were now getting smacks as we tried to move away from the club. We swung like mad trying to get some vengeance, but it seemed everybody leaving the club, running our way, was laying into the two Skins they had already decided we were, or at least I was, from London and being Skins didn't help – and we must be with the *Rejects*, Punks, smoovies and herberts all having a go. By now we both were nearing just rolling up on the floor mode. My head hurt, my mouth hurt and I was still being kicked and punched. Fuck knows how the poor sods in the club had got on – they didn't have anywhere to go. Then the Plod arrived. Fuck me, they just ran straight past the multitude running our way, laying in the odd boot, and went straight into the club. Jesus, just to be nicked to be safe. Then a second lot came up the street and, thanks to them, the violence stopped.

Both of us just stood and looked at each other. "What the fuck happened there, mate?" I said. By fuck we were lucky.

By now, the two we came up with appeared – strange that – couldn't see them coming out during the running assault, but we didn't feel like arguing or asking. All we wanted to do was get home, back to camp and, as we started off towards getting back to the station, the ambulances were coming.

That night taught me a lesson or two: listen to your instincts. If it's not feeling good, don't stay. Also keep away from gigs that have a footy scenario in the background; it's just stupid. But that's what life is all about: learning lessons. It wasn't until a couple of days later that we found out the extreme violence that had taken place. People could have been killed that night, and even the band could have been killed. Because of it, the *Rejects* tour ended in farce. I think they had trouble at their next gig in Liverpool and the gig was cancelled – again football related, but I've heard stories since that a couple of the lads that were there got their own back on their usual Saturday football entertainment days. Inter City Firm never forgot and nor would *Cockney Rejects*. I never got to see them again, not even now on their comeback tours like so many bands. That night left a nasty taste in my mouth and a missing tooth as a reminder. But I liked the *Rejects*; their first album is one of my favourites and they stuck up two fingers to all politics. If I ever, ever get to have a chat about that night with the band, I would really like to know how they felt coming on stage. They must have seen that lot masking as Punk fans and the hate in their eyes. Anyway, a night to remember, for all the wrong reasons.

The Skull

As I've said, I served in the Armed service, Royal Air Force to be exact and, apart from still being a Skin and doing as I pleased, regardless of punishment, I enjoyed my service. But my brother and I were not the normal, average servicemen; we stayed Skin and behaved as they did in civvy street and looked forward always to meeting up with the firm when we came home on weekends or leave. I also collected oddities and one of those was a human skull, a real one. I'll not say who gave it to me, in case they are still involved in the medical world and get them in trouble, but, needless to say, the person whose skull it was signed his rights away to it, and I got it. What made things worse was that I had some rabbit fur and cut it up to look like a Mohican and glued it to the skull: fabulous, and then I got hold of some fluorescent green lights which are used on aircraft and glued them into the eye sockets; perfect fit and, as soon as night came and a light hit them, bang! Glowy green lights in a human skull. The skull used to sit on my window ledge, looking out, and for a time nobody took offence; it was a continuing joke on camp. The nutty Skin has a skull, but they didn't know it was real unless they asked.

Then one day we had the usual camp inspection, a top ranking officer would come round and check on a picked block to see if everything was clean and sparkly, and all acceptable. Well, unfortunately, our block was chosen, so he was taken around the camp, to all the places to run his beady eyes over and say yay or nay. Well, just outside our block he was looking round; now, I'm only told this as, being just a ranker, I was not outside with all the Zobs (officers). I was standing outside my room, awaiting the order for, "Attention, officer present." but it seems he looked up and his eye caught the skull looking at him. He just pointed and said "What is that?"

Well, he just made straight for the entrance with everyone following and made for our floor and my corridor. As he came up, the order was given, "Attention officer present." and all obeyed and came to attention, but he didn't look at anything or anybody, just made his way down at a pace towards me. I could see out the corner of my eye a mass of officers and the station SWO (The Station Warrant Officer, another name for God, a nasty man, whose rank I respected but he was a bully and vindictive). As they came towards me, I knew it was either trouble or a pat on the back. They came to me and asked to go into my room; in my mind I knew I would have no trouble with tidiness. I'm not being big-headed but my room was always spotlessly neat and tidy; he would need a microscope to do me for dirt, but I did know they would have a shock when they opened my door. As I opened the door and stood back, the visiting officer just stopped as he was going in. There was silence. I knew what he had just seen. As you entered the room the wall opposite the door was covered in WW2 propaganda posters from Germany, England, Russia, and the USA. As he stepped into the room and looked right, the wall was full of WW2 posters of aircraft and a banner I'd made that read, Terror From The Skies. Then his eyes went back to the window and the skull; by this time I'd been asked to enter the room with all the other entourage and the door was shut (no prying ears). Either side of the skull were two exhibition jars from a veterinary scientific exhibition of oddities, in which were the foetuses of animals: a two-headed pig and a rat with six legs (all these things were given to me by my dad; he worked for a government run experimental veterinary unit, all hush hush and I didn't ask how he got them. More oddities I'd donated to my School). The officer then turned left and, where my bed was, on the wall was a picture of all the then heads of state: presidents and prime ministers and dictators of the world, and a note saying *power corrupts; absolute power corrupts absolutely*. The visiting officer turned towards me; he didn't show any anger but the SWO and the station commander looked like someone had just asked to shag their missus. This was going to be fun.

"Are you averse to power?" he asked me.

Well, I was known for not pulling any punches, so I replied, "Only if it's wrong and corrupt, sir."

He turned his head; all was quiet. He looked back at my skull and oddities and said, "Is that skull real, and are those things real and safe?" and he was pointing to the window.

"Yes, sir, all real and safe... sir."

He looked at the other officers present, said the day was over, then said he was going to have a chat with this airman and the station commander, with the SWO and block officer to be present, and it was gonna happen then and there.

Well, at least nobody else had a visit and I was dragged along with the officers and led to the commanding officer's office; something like going to mount Olympus, you just don't go. But there I was in a room full of commissioned power, a nasty SWO and me. Again this could go two ways; I was either going to be shat on from a very high power or an in-depth talk and understanding would take place. It was an interesting chat. I was asked was I anti-Semitic. Well, the only Jew I have come across was a Skin called Mesha and he was okay. Was I a devil worshipper, (skull et-al). No, I'm not, but I'm not a Christian, either. I then told them the skull was given to me by a Doctor of pathology and the jars were genuine exhibition material – I just liked to have them in my room – none were stolen. Then he went on about the posters. I just said they were self explanatory. I had nothing against authority as long as it was equal and fair to all. While all this was going on, the station commander was also asking the odd question, both high ranking officers surprisingly being very calm and nice, but the look on the SWO's face was like a bulldog chewing a wasp; he couldn't wait for the nod from these two to march me out and bring down the full weight of the armed forces disciplinary procedures. He didn't like me and my brother and just wanted to be nasty.

Anyway, after about an hour of conversation, I had to agree to remove the skull and exhibits; they were not to Royal Air Force standards. Fair play, I understood that, but I didn't have to remove the posters; they quite liked them and they agreed I did have a story behind the pics, and they liked I had a tidy room. Result. They did ask, before the end of the interview, whether I was loyal? Well, I would die for what I believe in, not for a flag waved by rich people who would win no matter who won, and I'm not a Royalist; power and that respect is earned, not born with.

Well, that was that, marched out, a bit confused, thinking that was going to be my final days in the service, but I think respect was given both ways, and my room was always inspected from then on, and I always had something not the norm for them to look at. But the SWO got his ounce of flesh; he made a beeline for my room after the meeting and he went through all my kit and clothes, looking for anything to discipline me. Ha ha, mate, nothing, but he took a brand new DP, surplus jacket I'd just bought from an American Marine, he said it had to be checked against the issue number in case it had been stolen. It wasn't, but I never did get it back and I wouldn't give him the satisfaction of asking for it. I'd never plead to a twat like that, and I had my revenge. The day I left the service and was on the station waiting for the train home, he was there with a couple of his hangers-on. I just walked up to him, put my face very close to his and said, "One day, not too far in the distant future, I'm gonna bump into you again and I'm gonna kick the shit out of you and you won't have any of these twats next to you to hide you." I never did, but he got the picture, and to see the shock on his face made my day. PER ADVA AD ASTRA.

Disco

During the 80s if Skins went to disco's it was a joy to put on the tonic suits and loafers or brogues (yep, they were called disco's back then). It looked good and made a change! The music that was played for them was mostly some punk, Oi, or two-tone inclusive of *Madness* and *Bad Manners*; it seemed that all DJs played these bands and the same old songs to keep the peace. As you know, I'm not a two-tone fan, and I'm not knocking all the DJs, but they didn't have a clue. Maybe the odd one would put on Skinhead Moonstomp by *Symarip* or Double Barrel by *Dave & Ansell Collins*, and if there were Skins there that knew our history and loved Ska, then skinhead reggae or blue beat you would dance. The new breed that grew up just with punk and then two-tone would simply look on – it's easy just to jump around, but some Skins could actually dance, and even we who loved Ska would get a bit bored with the same old couple of songs being put on for us. Please, please, we would say, have a DJ who had more than the token two tunes and bloody two-tone.

In and around Stafford in the late 70s and 80s was a massive Mod scene; it was impressive, and with this were a lot of 60s and Mod disco's. We found out by chatting to a couple of Mod girls that there was a disco soon and they played a lot of our original stuff and it was local, Stafford's *Top of the World*, so we decided to pop along and take a look. That's if we would be allowed in. It was a Friday night. Dan, Bounce and I got into the tonics, loafers highly polished, and off we went downtown, all suited and booted and feeling A1. I can't remember a lot of the pubs' names now and no doubt the town has changed a great deal since we were there. I probably wouldn't recognise it at all, but we went into one that was near to the back of the church in the town centre, not too far from the station. I used it a lot; I knew a barmaid and got on okay in there. We had a couple of beers then around the road to the club; it looked like it was going to be a good night. We saw some lads and girls coming from the station, heading towards the club; they were mods and when we arrived there was a queue – so here we go – will they let us in or not? Fuck me, I don't know why we worried; we got there and were let straight in after the usual search, but no questions.

As we walked into the hall, had a few looks, probably because nobody had seen us in there before, and three Skins all suited and booted and outdressing some of the mods must have been a great sight. First order of call: get a drink, then a place to root and look good and cool. Well, what more can I say but, fantastic! Some other Skins came in, Mods, Northern soulies and people who just loved the music. The music was great all night; Bounce was over the moon with loads of Northern soul and he danced with the mods and Northern soul heads. I tried, only a beginner at throwing my legs around to that then. Dan was chuffed because they had two-tone, as well. He and Bounce were jigging away to that, and then they also had Ska, blue beat and some skinhead reggae. We all wiggled away to that. The Mods and Northern soul lot were great; they liked the fact that skinheads had come to the gig, and dressed up for it, and we had a fabulous time – but like all good things it had to come to an end.

We left hot, sweaty and knackered and, as we walked up the high street, there used to be a little Wimpy van, one of the first, very busy little place, stuck just off the road with a few seats. As we got near, we noticed a couple of Mod blokes sat on the bench in their parkas and a Modette, all in their late teens. Next to them, standing in front, were a bunch of blokes, four of them, probably in their late twenties. It didn't look nasty; it looked like they all knew each other. We were on the opposite side of the road and, as we got near, one of the four lads just turned his head and caught a look at us on the other side of the road. Without hesitating, he shouted Mod wankers and gave the wanker sign with his hand, then turned his head back towards his mates. Well, we just looked at each other and behind us, in case there were others there; then Dan said, "He's talking to us," and started crossing the road.

Oh fuck, I thought. Bounce and I followed. All I wanted to do was get back to my room; I was knackered and smelly. As we were crossing the road, I was trying to tell Dan that it wasn't nothing and they were pissed up idiots – let's just get home and not nicked.

Bounce and Dan had gotten instantly into arguing mode, so I just followed. As we crossed the road and got near, we saw one of the four in front of the mods slap one of the lads across the face; the girl was crying and it didn't take a professor to work out these three were being set upon by the four piss heads. By now we had crossed the road and were nearly next to them, coming up from just behind them. The one who had shouted turned his head and, without hesitation, my brother just smacked him in the side of the mouth and said, "We ain't mods, I'm a Skin."

This was not a dig at mods, just a fact. As he did this, the other three turned round. Bounce had already picked a target and started to punch the shit out of one. I grabbed the other by the throat (I had to; it had all gone off, bye bye bed), and squeezed as hard as I could, pushing him away into the Wimpy van. The two mod lads saw their chance and scarpered at warp speed, except the girl; she had curled up on the seat. Dan was punching the shit out of the mouthy one. Bounce by now was doing the two step on his victim on the floor, and I was trying to throttle my victim when – wallop – the cheeky sod, who hadn't got into the fight yet, smacked me in the side of the head with a bottle – crack! – stars and glass everywhere. Remember, folks, all this happens very quickly, and you just have to take your chance and always be aware, but

I had an excuse. I was fucked, knackered and sweaty. I took my eye off the ball. Anyway, I went sideways, seeing stars. The one I'd throttled had gone unconscious through lack of air and had slid down the van to the floor. Dan was busy now two-stepping his victim and, thankfully, Bounce jumped into the one with the bottle, my head cleared and I just lost it. I've been hit again on the head with a weapon; it was not just because Bounce had struck the bottle user, but all I saw was a movement from him as he got off the floor and I just swung my leg as hard as I could, a fantastic contact, right in the side of the cheek – crack! – I knew his jaw had broken but all I saw was the sole of my loafer go flying through the air. But the bottle user was out cold, all done.

We now had to get away; there were others watching from across the road and the Plod would be there soon. We just ran, and I had only one good loafer, the other was just hanging around my foot, flopping all around my ankle, my white sock in tatters and I was pissed off. I had a headache again but, as you do, you just laugh with your mates after a fight like that on the run. I suppose it's the release of all that adrenaline, and you all talk at the same time, at twice the speed of sound about what had just gone on and the result of it all. Well, luck or the gods, we got back to camp. The next day on the local radio was a report about a fight in town and four lads had been set upon and hospitalised. We couldn't fucking believe it; someone had made up a story again, got it all wrong. We went to help three innocents getting picked on. Well, there you go; the only result was they said it was mods picking a fight after the club had finished. We didn't know if that was good or bad. No, it was three A1 Skins on a mission of help, but I had to buy new loafers and we all had to have our tonics washed twice to get rid of the blood spatter, and we never ever knew what happened to that Modette; she was pretty.

Family Outing

1981: It was all the family: Mum, Dad, aunts, uncles, brothers and sisters, cousins and some friends. We had all clubbed together, hired a coach and were going to spend an all day'er at the seaside (Weymouth), drinking, eating, and in the arcades, having a laugh, and considering the amount some of the family would drink, it *would* be a laugh.

We all met at a pub called *The Carousel* (it's gone now, pulled down and a scummy drug den is there in its place), a complete coach load. Mums and Dads stood around in their headscarves (the women) and the men in their out-dated leisure suit jackets. It was gonna be a warm day and the women were still in their long coats and headscarves. Oh how I miss that look. The younger lot, cousins, et al, were stood around chatting and already starting on the beer that was brought along, (at this time crates of beer were still allowed on coach trips). We had a few crates, long day, we would be drunk. Dan, my sis, Tania, and I were all Skins. We were always the centre of attention – what have we been up to, yard, yarda, and the cousins et al didn't have the bottle to do the same as we did.

Also my sis had brought along her boyfriend: a Punk. He was about six foot one and the skinniest bloke we had ever met. A massive black and white Mohican – at its highest it was fourteen inches high – stood there in his leather jacket, one arm covered in studs and the whole back of the jacket studded, black bondage trousers tucked into a pair of Docs too big for his legs as he was so skinny. Problem was he had massive size thirteen feet, so getting boots to fit was hard enough, but because his legs were so thin the boots would wrap around them. Thank God he tucked his trousers into his boots; at least that filled some of the gap. His tiny waist had this belt he made himself that held his trousers up, covered also in pins studs and chains. HIS NAME WAS CLARENCE – YEAH, CLARENCE. Who the fuck would name a kid CLARENCE during the the late 60s, early 70s – the only Clarence I knew was a crossed-eyed lion from a series called *Daktari*? And boy, was he thick? You could talk to him for hours and nothing would stay in his head, but he was a genius with instruments and music. Give him an instrument; he would be able to play it within twenty minutes. He would listen to some music once and remember how it went, then play it. It wasn't till later in life we found out he had Aspergers; that's why he was a genius with music. Okay, he was a Punk, but a bloody good one. He wasn't a poser, but they did look funny together – six foot one Punk and my sis was four foot eleven – and that's pushing it some.

Coach turned up and we all got on. Some crates of beer went in the coach's luggage holders and some came on with us. Back of the coach we took over all the young ones. Now we could get drunk on the way. The plan was to get to halfway stop, have a pee and maybe a sandwich and then carry on to Weymouth.

All was going well until BANG,WOOSH! Two of the vents on the roof of the coach pinged open, nearly coming completely off the coach roof. Panic and mayhem from some of the elder trippers: nans and granddads. All the women grabbing the headscarves that are still on their heads, the men grabbing their hats and caps. Luckily we were not too far from the stopping place, and the coach slowed down to save its roof's vents and we pulled into the service station, taking a parking place away from other coaches so the driver could look at the damage and assess what action to take. On the trip was an uncle who was just a genius with car engineering, so everyone called him up.

"Olly, have a look – can it be fixed?"

The driver just looked down, shaking his head; he already had doom on his face. A good driver but no knowledge at all of engineering.

All the coach party now went and stood about fifty feet from the coach to stare and point. Olly, by now had looked from the inside and said it needed to be done from the outside on top. Well, Dan and I had heard this and, being a tad tipsy, climbed on top of the coach, my missus giving me orders not to be stupid and be careful, (yeah, right. I'm tipsy and Dan and I have gone into 'go' mode). Olly knows what's wrong — then comes the bad news, NO TOOLS. It needed to be banged back into place, but without tools.

Dan and I looked at each other and the first thing in both our heads was FUCK TOOLS, WE GOT BOOTS. We went straight into action; we both took a vent and started jumping on both of them. Fuck it if they never opened again — we wanted to get to Weymouth. My sis and her boyfriend were standing by the coach door, giggling and pointing at Dan and me. The family were also pointing and snapping pictures; the driver had turned around, crouching with his head in hands.

While all this was going on, we didn't notice cop cars coming into the car park, loads of them. SCREEEEECH! Sirens on as they pulled up by us: two car loads and a meat wagon, coppers everywhere. They ran over, grabbed my sis and her boyfriend and slammed them up against the coach. At the same time they were shouting at Dan and me. We were completely oblivious to what was going on, too into jumping up and down on the roof. Next thing I saw was a hand grabbing Dan's leg and pulling him off the coach. He gave a shout.

"OI, FUCK OFF!" And then a screech as he came off the roof.

As I turned to go to his aid,"GOT YOU!" YANK — a copper pulled me down too. We were both slammed up against the coach.

"YOU'RE NICKED, YOU'RE NICKED!" is all we heard from the plod.

This had now infuriated my Mum and Dad who, with a few of the other uncles and aunts and my Nan, were now turning on the plod. Complete mayhem ensued: pushing, shoving, swearing, and shouts, the driver coming up to the plod, hands out, shouting "What's going on?"

with terror on his face.

"STOP, STOP!" My sis was trying her utmost to take on the plod – a tiny terror she was. Clarence, the poor sod, was just up against the coach with a blank expression. I don't even know if he knew what day it was, or even if he would remember his name if asked by the plod. Dan and I, as by norm, after being slammed up against the coach were having a go back at the plod. This led them to handcuff us and us being thrown to the floor, which then upset the family even more. After about ten minutes of swearing and confrontation, stability ensued. What the police told us was that someone had gone to the staff in the service station, after seeing Dan and I on the roof, and told them we attacked a coach load of oldies; they then called the Bill. This is the story I've told you; the plod appeared and in their usual way didn't ask questions just ploughed into the four of us. MUST BE NASTY – Skins AND Punks.

Our twenty minutes stop had by now turned into a couple of hours and a fight with the plod. We were let go but warned of OUR BEHAVIOUR to the police and that we could have been done for being drunk. So could a load of oldies as well. It would have looked good in court, all us lot; that would have been a laugh. Needless to say we all got back on the coach, angry, but pleased we were not nicked and Dan and I had done the repairs – ish. Well, we just gave the top of the coach a kicking – what fun. Except Clarence, who still didn't know what was going on; all he wanted to do was get on top of the coach, but we all had a great day in Weymouth, got very drunk and had loads of fun.

1981-82 Guide Dog Trainer

As I don't go down town very much now, or stand on the street corners, I don't know if the town centre still has the guide dogs for the blind being trained around the town. Back in the 70s, 80s and early 90s when I used to go to town a lot, I saw them all the time and we got to know some of the trainers.

Dan, me, Rich Q (I think) Simon, Shorn the Punk and Beak met up in town about 10.30ish, as always, on a Saturday morning. We headed for the local tea stand round the station and had our bacon roll and a cuppa. The ladies that worked there loved all us lot: special big rolls filled with extra bacon and we always gave them good service and kept an eye out in case they were ever in trouble from drunks. All fed, we decided to knock the pub up where we used and have a couple of beers, which we did, in the pub until mid-day. We then trotted off to see who was about.

As we came round to a place called *Quicksilver,* it was filled with arcade games and slot machines, right next door to a cinema in Friar Street, we saw a load of others: Skins and Punks, about twenty of them just sat about outside the cinema and Quicksilver, just dozing and posing as we did on a warm summer Saturday afternoon.

As we were waiting at the traffic lights to cross the road, the local guide dog trainer came up beside us: a young lady and the traditional golden retriever dog. She wasn't scared when we all noticed her and the dog, (they were used to us by now) petted the dog (I know it's wrong but they are fantastic) and nice chat with the lady before the lights changed and off they trotted, we following, making for the mass ranks of Skins and Punks. Again, as the guide dog went by, the parting of the Red Sea happened from the nastiest people in the town: us lot. Everyone saying hello and with total respect. I think the local shoppers, et al, were amazed to see us lot show that much consideration and for the trainers to chat to us. There you go — we do have some morals.

We had sat about having a chat and a laugh, scaring all the public. It was late afternoon by now and we were just thinking of all going our own way, when one of the punks, Shorn D, said, "What the fuck is going on there?"

We all turned to see, outside a pub called *The Bugle* one of the Guide dog trainers with a blind man and the new probably guide dog this man was going to have, surrounded by four men, probably in their mid twenties. They were teasing the dog and taking the piss out of this blind man. The young lady in her yellow tabard, the trainer, had her arms out trying to get these lads, who were obviously drunk, to stop. The general public were just, as usual, giving a wide berth, staring but not saying anything. Then one old lady had the courage to wave her finger at these idiots. Well, that was too much for Shorn. All we heard was, "FUCK IT!"

He flew across the road. We followed *en masse*. Well the Skins did with the other Shorn the Punk in tow. Crash! Shorn D took one straight out, then we all took the other three: fist, boots, and head-smacking into these blokes. We managed to avoid the little old lady who, so we were told, had a great big grin on her face. The trainer and the blind man and dog were escorted out of the way by some Skin girls. These four, though, were by now getting the full treatment. I suppose the beer, the sun and sheer anger with these got to us. Plus, let's be honest, we were Skins and we liked a bit of fisticuffs (back then anyway). It was messy. They went down and were laid into by about twenty pairs of Docs and steelies. I suppose it took no more than forty seconds to get the job done. Then we all stopped and gave them as much abuse as we could, but then the self-preservation mode kicks in. Oops, Bill any moment. Off we went in as many directions as we could, except the Punks who had just watched from the *Quicksilver* steps, not a care in the world, still faffing about, but were giving us the applause.

All of us who took part in the attack got away, but those poor innocent Punks outside the Arcade were steamed by the Bill. Totally innocent they were but, as usual, the plod just steamed in without finding out what happened. Luckily for them, the little old lady and the trainer gave the Bill the true story of what occurred. "Those blokes started it, the Skins came to our aid and those Punks had nothing to do with the incident."

But the local paper got the story and made out we had done our usual mindless violence on four innocent blokes out for an afternoon drink. How the media works when you're public enemy number one.

We were also stopped from congregating outside the Arcade. If we were there for more than five minutes, the plod were called and we were moved on or nicked for vagrancy. But one thing good to come out of it: all those blind dog trainers knew that if we were about they were looked after and respected. And, of course, a nice smile from some of those lovely lady trainers.

5/11/1983 Reading University

We had been waiting for about two weeks. PIL, *Public Image Ltd* were going to play at Reading uni, we had accidentally found out. Well, we as a cult were not really wanted at the uni gigs; a bit fearful of us and we were not welcomed, but the day had come and so off to the gig. My brother Dan and I walked up to a pub not too far from the uni; it was always used by students and the local beer swallowers. Just outside the pub we met a few others; Richard Q, Black Jason – yep, a black Skin, Rich T, Ronnie, and some of the Skin girls. Also there were a few of the Punk lads that always hung around with us. We were all good mates and were always in the company of the others.

We had a couple of beers and talked about the coming gig. I'd had seen PIL about a year and a half earlier so I knew what to expect. For a lot of the others they had never seen PIL or the new Johnny Rotten or by his real name, John Lydon, so a tad bit of excitement, and of course a night of taking the piss out of the students – just had to be done. We left the pub for the ten minute stroll to the uni, knowing there would be some more of the Skins, Punks, and Herberts there. There was not a big queue to get in, but the normal search for weapons as we entered. Strangely, only the Skins and the Punks that were with us were searched, but even back in the 80s we were used to being searched on entry; there had always been some dick that took a knife or whatever to a gig; it happened then and it still does now.

As we all came through to the hall where the band was to play, we noticed a large group of psychoBillies, {Billies we called them}. This was not the norm; they usually didn't come in such large numbers, but we nodded to a few we knew and mutually went to the part of the hall that would become home for the two gangs: both groups getting disturbed looks from the students and the other nobs who just came to see Punk groups to boast to their mates in the pub or at work.

The evening started off as all Punk nights do: the band came on and – BANG – the music started after a torrid speech from Lydon. Everybody went mad: the norm for Punk gigs, bashing, jumping about and having a laugh. As I took a respite bite from jumping around, a hand grabbed me and pulled me. I turned around to see a stunning girl {Punk} with blonde hair smiling at me.

"Yes," I said.

"Hello, I'm Lindsey from Guildford. I've seen you around town {Reading}. I've wanted to say hello but didn't have the nerve." She looked at me with eyes to die for and a stunning body and face, {the fishnets and short skirt helped}.

"Well, you said hello," I said,"what's wrong?" as all around the hall people were going mad and music blaring.

She waited for a few seconds {which seemed ages} and then said, "Do you want to come outside and get hotter?"

I was taken aback by that. I stood opened-mouthed and realised what she said and looked at her. She tilted her head to the side and gave a fabulously sexy smile. Oh God, she was stunning and yep, I would have, but just as I was going to reply, "I'm married," I saw Jason rush past me with a growl. I looked to where he was running to with fist clenched. There in the mist of a gang of Billies {psychoBillies} was Rich Q and my brother giving what for; punches being thrown, kicks and blood everywhere, wallop. Jason joined in, escalation. I just ran in to the battle, punching and trying to pull the three of them to safety. Oh God, were they and myself outnumbered. Okay, some more of the lads that came to the gig with us came rushing over; for that minute we were holding our own, but for how long?

As we took our side of the hall, we saw some of the innocents who were standing in the wrong part of the hall getting up with nosebleeds or holding their heads, pointing at us or the Billies. The music had not stopped and plenty of people were still jumping around oblivious to what had happened, both gangs now eyeing each other up, and now I realised how many there were and why they were so cocky. Numbers count and we were outnumbered in the hall probably three to one. Oops, oh fuck, I thought.

"What the fuck happened?" I asked Dan.

"Well, me and Rich were jumping about..." Rich was nodding his head and agreeing with what Dan was saying, "and having a laugh with the Billies, but this twat got stupid and threw a punch. Well, me and Rich just started thumping back."

"Yeah, that cunt started it," Rich said, pointing to a Billy with blood pissing from his nose and mouth.

"Well," I said. "Gather everybody up and bring them this side and warn any going to the bar or toilet." Needless to say, the rest of the gig was spent watching each other and not taking very much notice of the band, and apart from that the stunning Lindsey had disappeared, and I never ever saw her again, EVER.

The gig got near the end, and we got everybody together to make the short journey to the exit. There were only a few of us together in the passageway: Dan, Rich, Jason, and a Punk, Sean Doyle {and when he got drunk walked around all the time with the best impish smile imaginable} and I was in front. Then in the tight space just coming to the door, the Billies attacked. Where they were hiding I'll never know, maybe a tad too drunk to notice, but they aimed for Dan and Rich, and came at them from two sides with numbers.

Jason and Sean,who were behind Dan and Rich, joined in straightaway and, as I heard the noise, turned round and instantly attacked. A massive scrum took place; innocents and students trying to get out of the way and both sets of gangs tearing chunks out of each other. Because of the way they attack, our little cohort had been pushed to the door. Thank fuck we held our own but had taken a kicking because of the numbers, but luck was on our side. As I looked to the door, I saw some of the Wrens that were with us had gotten outside and had made contact with our latecomers and lo and behold there were loads of local Skins and Punks from the town waiting for us. They were too late to get in and were taking the piss out of the students while listening to PIL outside the hall. Brilliant, I thought. As I got near the door they saw what was going on and got ready for the command. As we were pushed, punched and kicked outside, the Billies thought they had us; they charged out to meet our back-up.

"AVE EM!" I said and the charge took place; it was fucking great, like Custer's last stand. As they came out they were attacked, and as the fallen tried to get up the birds were in straightaway – some really great bootwork. I don't know how they do it but it seemed seconds before the Bill turned up: cars, vans, dogs, the whole lot, but to our luck they came in behind where the psychoBillies, who were trying to regroup, were and being nicked. We made a hasty tactical withdrawal to the other end of the uni field, in the direction of home.

Now it was time to take stock and see who was hurt and who had stayed or mysteriously gone missing {We all had Skins and Punks that talked the talk but never walked the walk}. Dan and Rich were showing their attack; they would have bruises for sure, and it was a relief they were just bruised. Luck was on their side, well honestly speaking, on all our sides. We were lucky – fucking good fight but lucky. That's how massive rucks happen; not just how hard you are or think you are, numbers count and the amount of nutters you have within those numbers. It did help on that night when they attacked. All that was trapped for that short time were in the mould of nutters, that code of honour, no retreat no surrender, stand by your mates, Dan and I lived by that, and we have the scars and injuries to prove that many a time we had a kicking because of thinking of others rather than self preservation.

1987　The Red Cow

Taxi-drivers' revenge

We went to the pub on our usual Friday night drinky, to start our weekend, re-fuel from a week's work. The night went quite well: no probs, a few of us in the pub, and some of the younger ones hidden round the back, out of sight, out of mind. Another case of at least it is money for the pub. Lots of beer had been drunk and very tipsy we all were. My brother, Dan, was with his Swedish girlfriend, under the pool table doing what you do with a good-looking girl, nobody taking any notice. Well, it would have been rude, wouldn't it? Anyway, it got to about 10:30pm and I thought I'd go get some chips.

As I walked to the door to leave, all I saw was Andy J backing up and a load of foreign language and fist swinging at him. The noise had alerted everyone else and, as I came to his aid, my brother and the mob came to ours. It seemed something had happened in town with a Paki taxi driver and they were out to get any Skins, and they knew where we drank. It wasn't hard; we used their taxis. The rank was fifty yards up the road. Anyway, more and more cars pulled up and Dan, Bristol Dave, Mark C, Grainger, Simon, Andy J, Sawyer, Squid, and I had a battle on our hands. Even the girls: Wendy, Nikki, Marina, Debs, and others had jumped up for the oncoming battle. All the pool cues were by now in our hands and a battle by the small entry/exit door was on.

We were outnumbered, but if we lost this and they got in, we would probably get a kicking, so anything went, all trying to get as many swings in with cues and kicks, hitting each other in the process, trying to ignore that pain, and trying to stop the horde that was trying to get in. It was messy, loud and painful, and then the knives came out:

THEM not us; jabs and stabs at whoever was too close, and I think everyone there had some wound from them.

Then, without any warning, glasses and bottles came over and through our phalanx. The girls had armed themselves and started lobbing the missiles. Grand idea, but women {sorry, ladies} can't throw or aim, but it helped. Anyway the fight had seemed like it went on for ages and the only way of getting any result was to charge – the last stand: charge, victory or death, a shout and then go, straight into anything in front – if it's not a Skin, hit it. This caught them off guard; they didn't think we would attack their numbers. They retreated and looked stunned. As they did this, the local plod arrived in numbers, {sometimes I thought they had instigated all this because of the speed and numbers that arrived} the taxi drivers, who could get away quickly, zoomed off. The others just gave a load of unintelligible crap and pointed.

We, on the other hand, just threw everything we had in our hands back into the pub, bleeding, bruised and in pain, we pleaded innocence to the plod, waiting for the usual "YOU'RE NICKED!" Well, we were always to blame, weren't we? But to our surprise, a bus driver who had to stop because of all the cars that pulled up, and our landlady had come to our defence. We weren't nicked – just the usual search and names taken, {thank fuck none of us had our chains on that we wore at times}.

The doorway to the pub looked like a bomb had dropped; glass bottles, window glass, bits of pool cues, blood, beer and snot everywhere. We had stood again and won. Fuck me, that was close, and if they had just stopped and thought about their attack, they could have had us. Behind where we held them were two more entry/exits; all they had to do was come in all these at the same time {they had the numbers; it worked against them}, we would have got a kicking. We found out later that the trouble started because a man with short hair had refused to pay the driver and done a runner towards where we drank. So 2+2 = 5 – had to be a Skin didn't it, forgetting we had used their cabs for the last year or so with no problems?

Expecting now to be barred again from the pub, we went back in to retrieve our coats and bits. As we left, we apologised to the old landlady and expected the usual "you're barred lads", but she looked at us and said "They were to blame. Thanks for looking after the pub. See you tomorrow night." Ye-hey, result – someone who understood what went on. It didn't last long. Not long after, the local Race Relations Board got involved and made a plea to the local council and Police to have us kicked out of the pub because it caused friction. "Well, thank you, multi-cultural England." One law for them, another for us....AGAIN.

1988 Pub Fight

Saturday night, the wife and I were going to meet up with some friends: a couple of Mods, Ian and Linda West {great people, good Mods} and Keith and Sam. We were all going down to the pub {Red Cow} to meet my brother Dan and his French girlfriend. It had been a good afternoon; I'd had a few beers and had watched the six nations rugby {five nations then} game, France v England. England had lost but that wasn't a shock, and I've always been a rugby and cycling fan, so I didn't take this result badly. England were shite.

A brand new pair of white sta-press I had; they were really nice, not some of the thin material you get now to rip us off, but pucker lovely. Decided I'd take them up for my boots and not shoes; it just looked better. Also a brand new Brutus; I think it was a green and blue colour check, so I felt really good.

Keith picked us all up and we went down to the pub. As I walked in, there was Dan and his girlfriend sitting at a table midway into the bar. At the same table was a bloke looking at Dan and he had a friend who was looking up at the TV, which I didn't know at the time, these two were together. I was the first of us in the pub; my missus followed me, then Ian and Linda, Keith and Sam.

They must have just seen a flash as I walked in. I saw my brother swing at this bloke and just instantly flew into attack mode. I ran over to thump the bloke; as I got near, his mate grabbed me by my arms. I automatically threw my head back: crack! Caught him straight across his nose and jaw. He just dropped blood, snot and tears. Meanwhile my brother had gone for this bloke again — more haymakers aimed at him.

Then I saw how big he was: HUGE, but they didn't call Danny pit bull for nothing. He was at him with gritted teeth, but a blow came at him straight and true, caught Dan on the head and sent him backwards over the chairs he had come from. This was all happening at speed; the others were still just walking in.

My missus had seen this sort of thing before; she instantly moved at speed out of the way. The Mods that came in with us took a tad of time to see what was happening; meanwhile I'd attacked this bloke with a couple of smacks to the head, and my attention was lost for a nano-second as Danny's girl friend had blasted the man with French torrents and proceeded to slap him on the head at a hundred miles an hour, her hands going up and down on his head. It just was a stereotypical girl slap she was doing; he probably didn't feel it but the thought of it now does make me laugh.

Anyway, as I proceeded to try and dodge his retaliation, all I saw was this blur come from above me – CRASH, a massive pot plant hit him. My brother had gotten up, picked up this giant pot with a plant in it, jumped up and planted it straight on top of his victim. Blood just sprayed everywhere, and he slumped to the floor with me still hitting him, but we just stopped, as he sank to the floor out cold. He had this mound of dirt on the top of his head with a massive plant still in it; it looked like it was growing from his head. Before we could get to him with boots, my missus pulled me away and the others got Dan.

"HE IS OUT OF IT. STOP YOU TWO, YOU'LL KILL HIM!" But everyone who was a Skin knows you don't think of that – just the thought of victory is all you're interested in. The bad side comes later, often too late. But he was picked up, dragged outside and just dumped, still with the plant on his head and still out cold. His mate who had gotten up didn't want any more and went outside too, but instead of helping, just ran off. I don't know who phoned an ambulance, but he was taken away.

We later heard he had a fractured skull and jaw and was in hospital for a while. I also found out the argument and fight started over the England and France rugby game. Dan was like me; if England were shite and deserved to lose, so be it, but this drunk had insulted the French {I know they're French but c'mon, even Englishmen have to stand by them now and then} and my brother's girlfriend, and had taken Danny's small size for granted —a mistake he paid for.

My night also ended early; when all the dust had settled my nice brand new sta-press were covered in blood, plant life and some kind of fertilizer. Stern look from the missus, "WELL THIS NIGHT ENDED EARLY... AGAIN," she said and as we left I knew I was in for a bollocking when we got home, but in our defence, we didn't start it, and I knew I had to ask her to wash the sta-press as soon as we got in, a dodgy night was to be had.

Poll Tax Riots

On March 31st 1990, Dan, Bristol Dave, Ray Gun, Simon and I, had decided we were going up to London to watch the boat race and have a laugh at the expense of all the students and Hooray Henrys. Well, it was just a laugh, wasn't it, and some of those student girls were A1? We decided to go to London on the train, which was different, as we usually went by bus, got off at Hammersmith and all walked to where we wanted to go; then, like the multitude, got on the shitty underground.

We had no problems; got on the train at Reading and headed for Paddington. When we got there we all noticed, on the train and then walking about the station, groups of very strange people. Yeah, there were the bods going to do the usual London shopping, work and the ones going to see the Boat Race, but there were others walking around with rolled up flags, dressed in black or some combat gear and carrying backpacks.

We just all looked at each other and wondered: what's all this about, have we walked into some Commi march or something we didn't know about – could be dodgy? Then we saw some other Skins standing outside the *Pride of Paddington* pub, and walked over to them. As we got near we noticed one of them had a massive lump on his forehead the size of a golf ball. We asked what happened and how did he get that. They told us they were from Norwich, and had come down to London to meet mates in Carnaby Street to buy clothes (I don't think *Last Resort* was open then). As they were walking through Soho to get to their destination, a group of about twenty bumped into them in one of the back streets. They were all dressed in black or DP's (disrupted pattern army surplus); they just attacked them with flag poles and bottles, screaming, "You lot are dead this afternoon."

The lad with the lump on his head had been hit with the flip-top bottle of Grolsch. Well, if you knew that bottle, you knew how hard it was, and thank God it didn't explode on him, he would have been a mess. They then decided to get back to Paddington just to try to contact their mates, and for safety. None of us knew about a demo march, anti racist or commi march, and we didn't think there was a right wing march, so we didn't know what these bushwhackers were on about, but the ten of us now all stood together.

Outside the pub we could see a lot of strange individuals getting off trains and going down to the Underground. We decided to go to Carnaby Street with the lads from Norwich, now there were ten of us, so if we were attacked at least we could stand our ground. This time there was no attack, so we got to the destination and aimed for *The White Horse* in Carnaby Street. As we walked down to the pub, the others were waiting there, only three of them, sitting outside with pints, and all from London. Yay, they must know what's going on.

When we got to them, the normal banter took place: we introduced ourselves from Reading and then they asked what had happened to the lad with the lump, which I thought was getting bigger. The story was told again and then they said there was going to be a Poll Tax march. Thousands had come to London, and were going to march up to Trafalgar square; it was mostly normals, families, or nobodies, but they had also heard there was going to be trouble. There were anarchist and left wing groups, plus Class War was supposed to be organising something; they said they all had the heads up and were expecting something to happen. Don't walk around on your own was the order for the day.

As we were having this chat, the Old Bill appeared. In those days in Carnaby Street and the surrounding area, if more than five Skins were together, they would turn up and move you on, "Don't give us the same old story, you're doing nothing wrong, just move!" That was their speech and, unless you wanted to spend a day in the cells and a fifty quid fine, you moved. Well, thanks to the three London Skins who knew a pub not too far away that we could go in and have a beer which, of course, we did, as the day's clothes-shopping for the Norwich Skins had been ended.

We decided we would stick with this lot and have a beer – if we left about 2:30 we would still be able to get to the boat race area and have a laugh. Well, that plan was soon to end; the norm happened, the beer took effect, we lost track of time, and the more you drink the more silly ideas come to mind. It got to about 3ish and some bloke came in and was talking about the march, saying it was going mental, people being nicked all over the place and gangs of nutters, local thieves and Herberts everywhere, causing trouble. Well, like I said, too much beer and the thought of a laugh (and revenge for the lad with the Pluto size lump now), we all decided to go have a look. Little did we know it would become a war zone. As we followed the London boys to the target zone, Trafalgar Square, we could hear the noise coming from that area. Even though we were semi tanked up I think all of us were a tad nervous, what was all that noise? The sound of sirens was non-stop. As we approached, there was chaos. It was near 4 o'clock now and Trafalgar Square was crammed. There were thousands there and it was obviously going off on the other side of the Square. Well, with the beer inside and the adrenalin now up, we forced our way to the other side. It was near Cockspur Street where we caught the bus to come back to Reading. All the police were trying to stop the protesters going any further up, and also trying to stop them cutting through to get to Buckingham palace. Then we noticed that at the front of the crowd now were the people we'd seen at the train station; they were now all hooded up and some had phones or radios. They were shouting and pointing and others were running to the front of the protesters and organizing people to throw rocks and bottles and just go mental. How the fuck did they get away with this? If this was a skinhead rally or march we would have been followed and hassled all day long. Sometimes I wonder the strategy of the police; they don't take some crowds seriously until a problem starts. Again I think the phrase "judge a book by its cover", and we just had a bad cover. By the front of the crowd was a building and there was construction work going on, scaffolding up all the front and the builders were still on the supports, watching what was going on. Then we noticed some of the builders were chucking down lumps of wood and scaffolding on to a bunch of nutters; this was about to get nasty.

Then it happened. Although the majority of people there were innocent marchers, just there to sound off to Thatcher and her cohorts, they were caught up and – like anybody – sometimes you just have to look at what's going on and – pow! you get caught up in it. That's what happened.

Every nutter around London had turned up and were joining in with the hardliners that were at the front, or just stood back organising. They charged and attacked the Bill: bottles, bricks, the scaffolding and lumps of wood rained down on the coppers, then a charge. The Bill ran; who wouldn't? At this point they were greatly outnumbered. At the same time, any car that looked expensive was attacked and smashed, cop cars and meat wagons were also set upon. Then when the cops tried to come back with only a few on horseback, the hardliners attacked the cops and horses. They had darts and all sorts to throw at the animals. Well planned, to us lot, and we had been in a few messy fights and riots. That topped it, and I will be honest, although it was exciting and the adrenalin was up, we didn't join in. Still to this day, I don't know why.

By this time the London lads and the Norwich lot had gone their separate ways and fuck knows what they did or what happened to them. This had gone on for some time and, from our vantage point, we saw the Plod coming back in force. They lined up; they knew who they were going to nick (anybody) and anyone in the way was going to be a target for the baton charge. They did, and bodies were lying all over the place: men, women, young or old. We were just laughing and pointing at the poor sods who'd been hit. It was usually us, but not this day. Yet, I've heard since that people said the Bill were heavy-handed. No, wake up people, this lot that rioted were now on London streets robbing, looting, attacking cars and the Plod. How could the police regain the situation without a lot of violence and some collateral damage and, anyway, to see the odd journalist and TV crew get a hard slapping was good. They were good at making up stories about us on rallies, and now they couldn't get out of the way because they looked like the nutters causing all the trouble.

We decided to move away from this part of London before we were nicked just for being there. As we walked back up to the pub, there was some gang trying to smash in a shop window, with some coppers trying to stop it, but they were totally outnumbered. We had to get past to get away and head home, and as we made our way past, trying to avoid the Bill, in case they made a charge and just nicked us, one of the nutters turned round and swung a punch at my brother, shouting, "Nazi bastard!" as he did it. Then I knew it wouldn't be a straightforward tactical withdrawal to the station. Dan laid straight into him; his mates by now had turned round and attacked Dan – but they didn't see us.

Wallop! wallop! We attacked. This was stupid; there was a demonstration riot going on, there were bods looting and robbing, coppers everywhere and now these twats couldn't just carry on looting, they wanted to attack Skins. We gave as good as we got, and the Bill that was there just stopped and watched. I think they were scratching their heads, wondering what was going on. Now it was a riot within a riot. We went totally mental at this lot, toe to toe. Then from the corner of my eye I saw the Bill (now reinforced) moving in. I shouted the alarm. We didn't run because we were losing; it was self preservation from being nicked and, as were running up the road looking for the nearest pub or Underground to get away, I saw Simon carrying a massive box, it was a double cassette stereo.

"Where the fuck did you get that?" I asked.

"One of those dicks threw it at me, so I caught it," he replied.

What a result. He caught it on the run and still had it all safe. Sometimes I wondered if Simon had an angel watching over him.

Anyway, we made it to an Underground station, and back to Paddington with the trophy that Simon carried. The train was full of people with lumps and blood all over them, moaning and groaning about what just happened on their peaceful march. Well, norms, now you know how we feel. There is never a peaceful march in London; someone is always going to be against it and then that means the filth will be there. We just chatted all the way to Paddington, and then on the train back to Reading about the day. It had turned out very different to what we'd planned, but at least we were home with no broken bones or having been nicked.

To this day when people talk about the riot, I look at them. Were you there? No, you're too young. You didn't see what we did. There were people there to deliberately cause trouble, extremists to the core; their mission was to destroy and cause mayhem, and reading the papers the next day was great. No Skins or right wing extremists, just a load of posh students and hardcore nutters brainwashed into doing the same things we got brainwashed into, but there you go. The poll tax was and is a disaster; the old rate system worked better. This shit has just got the crooked politicians covertly rich, and to top it all for that day, we didn't know who won the bloody boat race, but I bet every Hooray Henry got pissed and had a good time.

A Few Funny Thoughts

As I've said, Dan and I had served in the forces, and one of the good things they teach you is cleanliness and how to iron your clothes and clean your boots, which we did and still do, but every time we went to town, Rich Q and D-day would admire the boots. They would go home and be at the polishing with vigour to top me and Dan; then as they would come towards us with massive smiles pointing to their clean boots, we would just point the toe of our boots towards them, gleaming they were.

Their faces would just drop "BASTARDS!" was a classic from them. "WEVE BEEN POLISHING FOR HOURS. WHAT THE FUCK DO YOU DO?" Well, it's top secret; bulling is a skill. Then told them, after you get the shine, we used to use clear polish for floors just to cover the shine and make it gleam like glass, as long as you didn't get it stood on, and it would crack sometimes. But it was one of those moments that you just had to be there to see their faces.

On another note, we used to go down to the river, loads of us. A few of us would jump off the bridges and just miss the boats. How we were not killed I don't know. I did eventually stop as I hit some metal underwater after jumping off at one time. Had gangrene in my foot that started tracking up my leg. Had an op to get rid of it. We also used to throw some of the Wrens in the river as well. I've recently found out from one of the girls I've met again that she couldn't swim. "OH FECKING DEAR!" I could have killed her, but Stella you are a wonderful girl, loved those run-ups and cuddles.

Mind the Silly String

When we came out of the Services we started work for a company called GKN VANDERVELLS. It was in Maidenhead and we were picked up and taken to work by coach. Loads of laughs. Rich Q and his Mum had worked there for a while, and later his lovely sister. He got loads of us jobs in the same place; there were lots of Skins there. You couldn't go anywhere in the factory without coming across ones and twos on any of the three shifts. Well that got rid of the view that we were all lazy, but one day waiting for the coach – Christmas time it was. Dan and I, Rich Q, et al were there just talking, when some of the others we knew came up to wait. As this bloke got close he pulled out a can of silly string. He stood in front of Rich and squirted; he covered Rich in yellow string all over his new Crombie. Without a word said, or any other movement, Rich's fist just sprang forward and WALLOP, caught him on his chin. "Cunt, look what you done to my Crombie!" before all went mad and we broke them up. Even though this chap was just joking, and the spray-on string wouldn't have done any harm at all, Rich would have killed him and probably lost his job, but needless to say no one came near the Skins with silly string any more.

Wedding

My wedding also had a few funny moments. I can remember being in the church. It was packed with the usual family and relatives, but I also had a church-load of Skins and Punks. As the Vicar came down the aisle he just saw all colours of the rainbow: spiky hair and Mohicans from all the Punks and a load of shaven heads in tonic and sta-press suits looking back at him as he passed.

My Dad said, "ALL RIGHT, VIK, HOW'S YOU?". Yep, Dad was drunk AGAIN and all the Punks and Skins just creased up, but the Vicar had a sense of humour and said, "WELL, THIS IS A VERY COLOURFUL MOMENT IN TIME." I don't think he had ever done or seen so many of our cults at a wedding; like everybody else he listened to the propaganda and believed we didn't do the right thing, like getting married, but there you go, media lies again. Anyway, as we all were told to sit, all was quiet.

Just as the sermon was about to start the door opened with an eerie creak. I could see the vicar looking up over the top of his bifocals. No one turned round at that moment until, chink, chink, chink, the sound of metal hitting metal was heard. I didn't even have to look round; I knew who had arrived: Kev Mcgrath. He was a dead ringer for Animal from *Anti Nowhere League* and even dressed like him with the two chains across his chest held in place by padlocks. And in with him came *Strangler* {Brian Wesolowski} in full bondage, his straps and chains clinking together. Everyone turned round; all that knew them nodded their heads and said 'okay' in whispers, but my Nan {God rest her soul} loved all the Punks and Skins, and being old and a tad nutty just said,"

OH, WHAT A PAIR OF LOVELY LADS, AND GREEN HAIR –
LOVELY."

This wasn't said nastily; she meant it, and as they both took their seats I could see the smile on the Vicar's face. Then from nowhere, as he was sitting, Brian said at the top of his voice {that was just how he spoke}, "HELLO MISSUS P AND MR P," to my Mum and Dad. We had all grown up together and he knew my parents and they knew him. We creased up; my Mum put her head in her hands; my Dad who, as I said, was already drunk, just turned round and said, "OKAY BRIAN? GOOD TO SEE YOU." Before they could go off into a convo, the vicar grabbed the situation and brought it back to the wedding, and that was that; he got on with the sermon, and we all had to listen to my DAD, yes DAD, sobbing through the whole wedding.

L-R: Denise and me, Ian West, Lin (bride), Dan and Beaker. All smart at Westie's wedding.

Pink Elephant

When Dan and I were on the run, we were in Stafford, a very rainy part of the world as I remember, but the people are down to earth and a great laugh. We got in with the local Punks Skins and Mods; we all hung around together and had loads of laughs. A family of Punks we got to know pretty well: two brothers and a sister, Hags, Gunge and I cannot remember the sister's name, but we were always together and had many silly adventures. We used to break into a scout/cum/cricket changing room at night time, after we had all gotten completely pissed and couldn't be bothered to find our way home; problem being with that it was in a local nut house, St George's I think it was called. And why have a scout hut/cum/cricket changing room on a field for nutcases?

Who knows the secrets of the local mental health authorities? I remember walking through the grounds one early morning, after a night of severe alcohol intake and, as we {Dan and I}, walked round a corner, there in front of us was a giant full scale elephant. Remember, we were on the nutcases' grounds.

"What the fuck is that doing on a seating area in the middle of a field for nutters?" Dan said.

I looked at him and shrugged my shoulders, then, as Hags and Gunge came round the corner — which one I don't know — said, "Look at the colour." Something in our pissed state and early morning tiredness we had missed: IT WAS PINK, a fucking full scale pink elephant in a nutcases' hospital ground? We just looked at each other and creased up. "HOW THE FUCK ARE THEY SUPPOSED TO BE LET OUT INTO

SOCIETY WHEN THEY GO BACK IN THE UNITS AND SAY THEY HAVE JUST SEEN A PINK ELEPHANT," I said.

Hags and co just smirked and chuckled. "Maybe they don't want them out, or maybe the patients don't want to get out, and if you have seen a pink elephant you ain't getting out." Well that's Pottery's local logic I suppose. Seemed a reasonable explanation at the time, but Dan and I often went to see the pink elephant when we were in the grounds and all etched in our names on the belly of the beast — like you do.

Waylaid by Nutty Ladies

We used to use a local hall which was owned by a church to do our band practice. This was about 1978-9. We would set up, do a couple of hours and go pay them for the hours we used to a house behind the hall. Yeah, we could've done a runner, but this hall was ideal and Punk bands {I say Punk as that's what we played; don't like the word 'Oi' and the band was a mixture of Skins and Punks} being given such a nice place to practise, with a stage, not a lot about, and it had a kitchen so the girls could make tea and coffee – a must for band practice; save the beer for later.

Anyway, I got the money from the others and went off to pay, knocked on the door and a lady came to the door.

"Hello Spike, come in, come through to the kitchen."

Off I followed, then realised, how the fuck does she know my name – never seen her before, or ever given her the money for the hall. As I went into the kitchen I saw the lady I usually gave the money to; they were both about in their 40s, not ugly, just a tad worn is the best thing to say.

The woman I usually gave the money to said, "This is my friend; she lives here too."

"Oh," I said, "How do you know my name?" I asked the the lady who had opened the door.

"We often come and listen; there is a room above your area. That's how we know your name."

Freaky, I thought; didn't know there was a room above us but, hey, at least they haven't complained about the noise.

"Wait there a moment," the lady who I usually gave the money to said. "We have just got to do something."

I cannot remember what it was, but both went out of the room. I sat myself down on a chair and waited. About five minutes passed. I was beginning to wonder what had happened when I heard them coming down the hallway.

"Okay ladies, heerrrrrs–" The words didn't come out. 'Here is your money' was still going round my mind as I looked at the women. One had removed her jeans and was standing there in her knickers; the other had undone hers and had pulled them open, "Okay, here is your money."

"We don't want the money today, we want you."

Call me stupid, but I just legged it for the nearest gap, into this room and closed the door: a tiny toilet. NO WAY OUT. Oh fuck, all I could hear was the ladies saying, "Don't be shy; we won't say anything."

Won't say anything? I was terrified they could be mass murderers. I just wanted to get out and have a beer. Bang, bang on the door and pleas to come out, and in 78-9 there weren't any mobile phones, so I couldn't see a way out of this.

"Okay ladies, which one of the lads has set up this good joke?"

"It's not a joke – you can have any one or both – we won't say anything."

By this time I was very scared. Yeah, I could have opened the door and had a quick double, but I didn't know if they were nutters; the loony bin we break into all the time was just ten minutes up the road and they might be day patients.

I looked up and saw a window; I stood on the bog and opened it. Thank fuck I could see one of the girls who came with us. "MUNCHHHHHHHHHH MUNCHKIN! " I shouted. She turned round to see me half out of the window waving like mad.

She came over. "What's up Spike?"

"There's two mental women in here with their trousers down wanting me to fuck 'em. Get me out. Get Dan —tell him to rescue me!"

She creased up. "Oh, mental Linda you met here."

"MENTAL? OH GREAT, SOMEONE COULD HAVE WARNED ME."

Off Munch trotted, giggling like mad, and thankfully got my brother and some of the others to come and help pull me out of this window. I had the piss taken out of me for ages, but I got out alive. Well those two were day patients at the hospital, so who knows what could have happened, and never again did I, or any of the lads {not so brave after all} pay for the hall; we always sent one of the girls. Well, we thought they would be safe, but after all they did say they wouldn't say anything..?

Cannock Chase

Dan, Taff, Bounce and I, all Skins, were with a bunch of girls on the Cannock Chase; Dan, Taff and Bounce were going out with three Punk girls. Dan was with Anna, Bounce and Taff both going out with girls named Debbie – seemed to be a very popular name in Staffordshire for girls.

We were on the Chase waiting for Anna's sister {they too were Punks and they were from just up the road Newcastle under Lyme} and a couple of friends. Dan and I, Taff and Bounce had never met the girls and Anna's sister before, so it was going to be an eye-opener; if she was anything like Anna {who was a stunner} it would be a pleasant meeting. The downer was that where we were all waiting was where the murders of three schoolgirls had taken place. Raymond Morris, the Chase murderer, so it was a bit eerie.

Anyway, as we were waiting we were having a couple of beers and a laugh, then we heard this noise. Let me put you in the picture; if you have ever seen any of the *King Kong* films, new or old, you remember the part when Kong first appears and all the trees and fauna being pulled up or pushed down – the sound of trees being pushed over – well that's the sound we heard. Dan and I just looked up towards where the sound was coming from.

"Oh that's probably my sister coming."

Dan and I just looked at each other; even Bounce and Taff stopped lip-wrestling and looked. Ooh dear, I thought. Then through the last part of the undergrowth from which the sounds were coming came this thing. YEP, THING came through, about five foot nine in height, very

98

big, about twelve stone in weight, wearing some *Wombles* type trousers, all furry and this great big full length Afghan coat. Canary yellow spiky hair and a metal bar that went straight through the nose. I mean straight through – the bar went from one side through the middle and out the other. This could not be happening – talk about two sides of a coin. Anna was close, on a scale of 1 to 10, to being 10; her sister wouldn't even get on the scale.

She came striding over, a big grin on her face, followed by two more Punk girls {not bad} and, yep, one of them was called Debbie; she came over and stood beside Anna.

"This is my sister, *Thingy*." {I can't remember her name, so I'll put Thingy}.We just looked at each other, waiting to see who spoke first. I gulped and said "Hello Thingy, I'm Spike; this is my brother Dan and that's Taff and Bounce."

Thingy said, "You talk funny, you sound like a farmer."

Okay, I thought, don't look her in the eyes or you will be in trouble, but the contact had already been made in her mind and she made a beeline to sit by me, (gulp). Please don't let us stay here on the Chase too long – anything can happen – and I still had the vision of those two nutters who tried to molest me, and we had a party to go to that night – it could be very nasty.

Anyway all things went well; she turned out to be a very nice girl, just that the ugly fairy had waved her wand over her. I must say though, I did see her tits one day and for her size she had great ones: total accident, at a party. I was going to the toilet in the night and she was laid out cold on her bed, door open and nothing on her top half. Well, it would have been rude not to look, but hands up, I kept very clear of her. But found out later that Taff had his evil way with her.

There were a lot of people I really got on well with in Stafford and I'd loved to see Hags, Gunge and their sister, also M; Anna and her sister, Tania, I think her name was; Debbie Rutter; Debbie Arnold; Debbie Neal; Helga {what a mixture, Irish and German} and

Munchkin, sweet little Munchkin. I've known many girls called Munchkin; they just get called that for being small, but she was special — a very good friend she was and a good Skinhead. What we know about vans and ruined houses Munch?

Some Other Mates

There are people who stand out; who made me happy to be around and always made me chuckle. Ronnie was one; Ronnie the plonker he was called, but not in a nasty way. I asked why he was called that from another old mate, Thom, or El Thomo as he was a *Madness* fanatic. He said, "Just look at his boots; they are too big for him and they wrap around his legs." They did too, which made me smile, but I liked Ronnie; what you saw was what you got and he didn't lie to me. He is still a character nowadays; another lad with an impish grin.

Another old friend I miss because I've not seen him in years is Simon. He, like me, at times walked around all clockwork at night. We got a good little crew up doing that: Simon, Paul, me and there was another chap, but I can't remember his name. Age, it gets to the old loaf. We used to go to a local pub, all sit round a table drinking milk and Malibu, all clockworked up – got you drunk, weird looks, but could be a tad naughty on the tummy. Yep, sometimes you and Armitage Shanks had hours of talking.

Graham Porter, an old Punk, was also a great laugh to be around. Dan and I had many adventures with him, getting drunk, parties et al, and, not only that, we worked together, so for a time we were pretty tight, and Graham was a 100 percent twenty-four carat Punk: great bloke.

Bristol Dave was a good bloke too. He lived at our house for a while and he was funny. Mark Kesler, also a great bloke – so funny, a natural comedian. Andy Benham {another good Punk} and the Doyles {brothers: Punk, Skins, and a Bowie fan, little Dave}. They were genuine people, and another good bloke who had or got an infamous name was Andy Frain. Dan and I met Andy, I think, in late '79. He was a skinhead, like the rest of us, got drunk, had a fight, went to football, yarda, yarda, but nothing like how the media portrays him now. I found Andy to be a very genuine bloke, quick witted with good repartee and a very good dry sense of humour. I liked him and still do, regardless of his football history. I don't condone what he's done, but it's the man not the legacy that I like. I don't care who thinks it's wrong to like him. Tough, he was a friend and hopefully he still is, even though I've not seen him for about twenty years. Maybe people will stop using him and he will then keep out of trouble. If not, just keep looking over your shoulder, Andy. There are plenty of people out there who would stab you in the back.

Another good Punk from then was a lad I grew up with: Brian Wesolowski, a very down-to-earth bloke. He got the name Strangler for a nickname, not because he had a vocation to strangle everyone, but was a massive *Stranglers* fan. I got him into Punk, and every time I see him, no matter who I'm with or he is with, he will tell them that I brought Punk to Whitley. "*He was one of the first.*" Cheers Brian, but there were one or two others. I just helped it along, and by late '77 I was a Skin anyway.

Mods

Let's face it, at some time, all of us, as skinheads, have attacked or harassed Mods. I even think every other cult of that time harassed Mods – it just wasn't fair. Even though I'm not a bully and have never liked bullies, I did give Mods some stick, as a young Skin. The older I got, the more I liked them and still do {my son's a Mod – bloody Mods}. But there were times we went a tad silly, especially when we saw two-tone bands. For me, like I said before, two-tone was for Mods. It was aimed at them more than us. Yeah, the odd song maybe, but I saw through two-tone.

One battle I can remember was when trying to get in to see *The Specials* at Basingstoke. It was messy all night; the poor Mods just took thump after thump, complete skinhead violence, and I can see why we weren't wanted at the gigs, but hey, the bands knew what Skins were, and they encouraged us in the early days to come. You don't bring a Lion to a party and expect him to purr all night. But then they did the wrong thing {as did *Madness*} and turned their backs on us.

But Mods I do like: the scooter thing, love them. Well, proper Mod ones: lights, mirrors, et al, great. Hate all the cut-down crap ones. Why? It's like taking a suit and shredding the trousers. Like I said, I like scooters, but I don't see the connection with Skins and scooters. I never saw my elder brother and his mob with them, and personally I wouldn't have one. IT'S Mod. But Dan, my younger brother, had loads, even a chopper one, which was done up by Hells Angels. They loved it, but again I suppose it's a personal thing. Everyone to their own. I did and still have loads of Mod friends and we have a laugh about some old times. It's a laugh when you can sit and have a chat and one will say, "Do you remember when those Skins attacked us at the traffic lights in town, and started kicking us on our scooters when we zoomed off?"

"Yeah, sorry about that but when you're young and that…"

But that didn't last long with me. Like I said I don't like bullies or being one and anyway I liked Mods; they were clean and smart, and the Wrens were lush. I like being around them and some of them are cracking dancers, and the Mod birds – yum-yum. Wish I'd had had a Mod girlfriend.

I am glad that of this moment in time {2014} there is a massive Mod revival going on. The Northern Soul scene is a growing underground one, and this is bringing more young people into the Mod culture, which will have an impact on us. Some will have a metamorphosis and become Skins, to keep us growing, and the fact that lots of the functions you go to will play along with their Soul is original Ska, Blue-beat, and skinhead reggae; all is good.

Bank Holidays

These weekends were for a time such a laugh, but as I got older the entertainment got stale and predictable. When I got into my 30s, during the 90s, I stopped going, and only recently have I had any inclination to go again, because of the reunions going on, and two of my mates, Paul and Anna, do a weekend disco {yes, vinyl back to 69 style} of music and get together at Margate and I want to go {if the missus lets me}.

Anyway, during the 70s and 80s went to parts of the south and south-east coast for a weekend's punch-up and laughs. Let's be honest that's what Skins went for, and usually we didn't stay more than one day. Well in my case I usually got arrested or put back on a train and told to go home. One comes to mind as it's one of the only times in my life I felt very intimidated and have to say a tad concerned with ours and my safety {I didn't let on}. Loads of us had gone to Southend,{Dan and I had loads of memories of the place, especially 1978-79. We did have loads of rucks in those two years – in the papers again}. We were going to meet others there and, of course, more Skins from around the country who would turn up. We got there as usual and had to have firstly some food. Good old fish and chips; even if not hungry you're at the coast, so has to be done. We pottered about having a laugh all day: funfair, find a pub, drink, then go round town looking menacing. Not bad for the day; no one arrested and all in good moods and feeling as you did, unstoppable. Well the evening went well, found a pub, a queers' one I think. We eventually got chucked out, tinned beer, laughs, and look at all the Wrens. God there were some tasty Wrens about, and the fact the girls with us were fit as well. We were now heading again for the sea front at night time, showing off the skinhead brothering, but during conversations we had learned trouble was brewing. Pockets of Skins were coming in, telling of a group of smoothies {West Street boys they called themselves, I think} from the local area, going round in cars and picking off Skins. Not too concerned – no one was going to attack a sea front full of Skins, not unless they have big and I mean BIG numbers. I can't remember what time, but the police decided we were not going to stay on the sea front and started shipping us, either out of the town centre or to the stations to send us home; some willingly went on their way, others were the official sacrifice to the bank holiday police-arrested numbers. The courts would be busy on Tuesday.

Like I said, lots had gone home. We started walking around – had to find somewhere to bed down. We started to notice a few cars going past, more and more frequently, all doing the same, windows down, wanker signs from the bods in the car, shouting at us, but not stopping. No trouble there; they stop, we do 'em, but they just drove past giving it the big'un. I don't know where we were heading, can't remember, but we ended up at a bus stop at the bottom of a hill.

There were about fifteen to seventeen of us: Dan; me; D-day; his missus; Julie; Wayne; Luke; Mark Cester; Bristol Dave; Louise; Lyn; Niki; Donna and Marina; Jenny; Debbie; Bridget and, I think, Wendy. We started to notice at the top of this hill, silhouettes – just a few, but more and more appearing. They were all coming out of the pubs, more cars going past, more abuse and at the top of the hill looking more menacing. Oh dear, this horde was now coming our way, not just a few now, fucking hundreds. It was like Zulu waves coming down towards us after skinhead blood.

The town's SPG {police} were by now out, going towards the mob, all in their meat wagons but they were giving us the wanker signs and abuse too. Fuck, I thought, we are in trouble, time to move. We got going at a steady speed and eventually found a pavilion. The mob were coming; we had to get inside and try to defend it and us. We managed to get in and one of the lads, Grainger, I think, broke up some benches and barricaded the door; the rest of us ripping off window closers to use as weapons. The mob had grown to silly numbers now; I think we all knew how people felt when they saw a massive mob of Skins approaching. Yep, this was dodgy, scary and we could all have had a serious kicking. The local Plod had just left us to our fate.

The casuals then attacked the pavilion; they also climbed on top of the shelter to try and get in, bottles, bricks, all sorts being chucked at the little fortress of ours. They tried the door, kicking and charging. We held it, giving some good smacks to anyone too close or who nearly came through. This went on for hours till about 2:30 in the morning; then they must have got fed-up or moved on. But it was time for us to move out and on.

We walked around for a bit and came across a block of flats, quite posh. I think it was for old people, but we got into the lobby and bedded down; some of the girls had brought with them their sleeping bags, so they would be warm, and the closer you got to them for warmth the better. We were knackered; the adrenalin had taken its toll – all that heightened activity and self preservation gets you mentally and physically. We needed sleep, but I think we all slept with one eye open. Any noise and bing! You were alert and awake, but once again, if you live by the sword you die by the same, and we were all fucking lucky that night, but always good now to chat with the peeps involved and have a laugh about it.

The story always changes – well, we are old, {I am anyway} and you have to indulge in storytelling. The thing I've always wondered about that night was the old bods when they woke up to find a lobby full of Skins. We didn't give them any trouble, except Dan and I stole a couple of bottles of milk that had been delivered. Well they were there, weren't they? I also think to myself, what if those casuals had got in, what if? What if they had set the place on fire? One of us or some could have been killed or seriously hurt; the police that night didn't give a fuck. We were the sacrificial lambs for the smoothies that night; a blind eye was turned and excuses probably already being made up if something had seriously happened.

The thing is, with the bank holiday violence came the journalists. We played right into their hands. After the violence of '77 and the fights of the '78 early bank holidays, the next two years we had journalist and film crews all over the shop. They would find a mob of us, supply us with booze and stoke us up, going on and on about 'Are you gonna cause trouble, yarda, yarda...' Yeah, we fell for it. They followed us around, waiting for us to kick off, then click-click-click, or the camera crew getting in close, filming the fights in close up. The next day's papers or the evening news would be full of FOUL-MOUTHED YOBS ATTACK THIS AND THAT, UNPROVOKED VIOLENCE FROM SKINHEAD INVASION ARMY.

We couldn't win; we were fools to ourselves, but when you're young and fuelled up with booze, who gives a shite? Only when you wake up in a cell, after you have slept off the beer: Oh dear, another court case and more fines.

Stoke Gig

The band had been booked to play in Stoke (so we thought). We weren't asked, just told. I can't remember who the other band was that we were to play the gig with. We were to meet up at the pub where it was to be held.

We had decided to hire a van to get all our stuff to the gig and, if we could, drag along a few mates, which we did. Mid-day on a Wednesday afternoon we left to travel to Stoke. Paul was driving, a friend both Dan and I had worked with for some time, and a goodly Skin he was. All the band in the van: Dan, me, Gordon and, I think, Stubsy, Debbie and Nicky; I think she was going out with Vince who was there with his sidekick, Jimmy, and Shorn Doyle, the Punk. That was all of us in the van. Jock Mcuan who was our drummer, the best we ever had, and his girlfriend were in a car and would follow us up to Stoke; they too had a car full of friends.

It wasn't a too eventful trip. We stopped off at a motorway service station and while some did legal shopping, the rest of us went on the five-fingered wonder and took whatever we could. It's amazing when you get back to the vehicle and see what others have acquired: food, that's okay, drink okay, but when you get someone who has spent the whole time pinching as many sweets as he could, it makes you think twice about their mentality. With a vanload of sweets and stolen pies and sandwiches, we continued up to Stoke.

Dan and I had talked Paul, who was driving, to make a stop in Stafford. We were going to see some old friends if they were still living in the same house. A great reunion: Agz, Gunge, their sister, Migly, were all there and we had a good chat. We also got in contact with another dear friend, Munchkin who, after a chat and cuddle, said she and her boyfriend would try and get to the gig. We said our goodbyes and continued up to Stoke.

This part of the trip was much harder. If you don't know Stoke, it's a warren: lots of little districts that make up the town, and we were to head for Hanley. I don't know what it's like now, but in the late 80s it was still old-fashioned and it took a while to find the pub.

We were the first band to arrive. We all got out of the van and entered the pub: deserted? Only two bar staff there; quite a big place but it was empty. Everybody just sat at a table while Dan, Gordon and I went up to the bar. We were getting funny looks; they could hear our accents and didn't expect a load of southern Skins and Punks to arrive in their pub.

"Where are the bands playing and setting up?" I asked.

Blank looks.

"We've been booked to play here tonight," Gordon said.

In a strong pottery accent, the girl behind the bar shrugged her shoulders and said, "Don't know anything about that. No one has told us."

We just looked at each other and Dan pulled out the booking bit of paper sent to us by the idiots we played for. He showed them the flyer that had who, with, where and when and we were playing at this pub tonight. Nothing – blanks looks still.

"Is the landlord in, or someone to talk to about this?" I said.

The bloke behind the bar got on the phone and a man came down the stairs and out into the bar to see us. In the meantime, Gordon had gone over to all the lot that came up with us and told them we were not expected. As he was saying this the other band came in: another Skin band, and Gordon was telling them about the fuck-up.

"Yes, lads, how can I help?" the landlord said.

"We have been booked here tonight," Dan said, shoving the booking slip into the landlord's face.

He looked at it, nodded his head, then said, "Yeah, had a conversation with someone about this about a month ago, but no one confirmed."

We just looked at each other and I think he saw the anger on our faces as we were taking this in. Two of the other band members came over and also heard the news.

All the landlord heard was a lot of southern Skins swearing and, as he looked over our shoulders, he saw at least twenty-five Punks and Skins now milling around the tables by the door, all with southern accents, albeit London and Berkshire ones.

"Okay lads, hold on – just follow me." He headed towards a staircase at the other side of the bar. As we followed he turned and said, "Bring that lot as well," as he pointed to all our entourage.

We gave a wave for all to follow and two bands and their support trundled up the stairs. When we came to the top of the stairs, it opened up into a big room with a stage in one corner, a set of drums already set up where a band could play and a bar the other end of the room. He asked both bands to follow him to one corner of the room and said,

"Look, wait here I'll see what I can do. There has been a fuck-up, but we'll see if we can sort this out." Off he went downstairs, leaving two bands looking at each other and a lot of Skins and Punks sitting around an unattended bar (big mistake).

Well we all had a chat, talking about who fucked up and what we were gonna do if we didn't play. As we were talking about this, our supporters and friends were heading towards the unattended bar – it just had to happen. We followed and, as we got to the counter, Jock McCuan had gone behind the bar and found a tray of cigars.

"Here you go," he said and started handing out the cigars – not single ones – in packets. Then he gave out the fag packets.

Well when in Rome... I got Shorn Doyle to hold his head under one of the pumps and pulled the tap: GLUG-GLUG-GLUG – it was on.

Yippee! How stupid can a landlord be – he had left close on forty Punks and Skins unattended in a bar and thought we would sit there with our legs crossed and playing charades. That was the waving of the starter flag; we had to have as much beer as we could before someone came back. As always you think of an instant plan. We needed someone at the top of the stairs to keep a watch out and give us a nod if anyone came back. Great plan if all went well. We gave some of the girls that job, some bottled beer from behind the bar and some chairs to sit on by the stairs. Great. Sorted.

Now get back to the bar and join everybody else. By this time, the bottled beer was mostly all gone and with different parties all over the room, Shorn the Punk had gone from head under a beer tap to head under an optic – well all the optics, now joined by others picking their favourite optic and downing as much as they could. Being careful had gone out of the window. Jock had issued everyone who smoked with their fags and cigars for that night and nearly forty Punks and Skins were upstairs in an unmanned bar with pints and bottled beer, whichever was your favourite, and having a good time. The only tap not used was the one that supplied Mild. No one drank that; it wasn't a southern drink, hardly sold in pubs even in the Eighties in Reading.

This had taken about ten minutes, when one of the girls shouted, it was like a bunch of school kids. We all ran to different corners, bottles being kicked under the chairs and pints being put out of sight, but everyone forgot the smoke. Cigar and fag smoke choked the room. These were the days when smoking wasn't banned; windows were being quickly opened if possible and bodies running all over the room with papers and magazines trying to clear the smoke. No hope; we were caught, as guilty as a puppy sat next to a pile of pooh. As the landlord came up the stairs, talking to one of his staff, he suddenly stopped talking and a puzzled look on his face appeared. The room was full of smoke; then a shocked look followed. We were all just looking at him, not saying a word, from all directions of the room, just shuffling our boots and acting totally innocent. He looked over to the bar where the only sound coming from there was Shorn laid along the bar. He was already wrecked: a massive grin on his face and giggling like a little kid (he did crack me up when plastered). It was a horrible tense silence. The landlord and his staff twigged straight away, but didn't really know what to do, or how it would turn out.

"Have you sorted it?" I said, as I made a move towards him, just to take his mind off what he thought had gone on and to find out if we were to play.

As he just looked around, taking in all the horror, he said,

"Yeah, yeah, I've got a sound engineer on the way with a PA, and there are people coming in as well already." The people coming in were Munchkin and her boyfriend and some friends – she had gotten straight on the phone to see who wanted to go see a couple of Skin and Punk bands playing.

Meanwhile, those staff who had moved towards the bar were looking at the empty racks of bottled beer, fags and cigars, and at Shorn sprawled along the bar top, considering what to do in case he just went mental. All other eyes in the room were turned towards the landlord. What he said now would mean either a kicking for him, or his tactical landlord skills would come to the fore and the situation would end peacefully for the moment.

He looked at his staff and said, "Get this lot downstairs and I'll sort out the bands."

Pheew – that was close – we might even get to play. We followed the landlord, who had a look of disgust on his face, but hadn't said anything yet. All the others, including the wrecked Shorn, were taken down to the bottom bar where, hopefully, they would now purchase their beer. Well that was the landlord's idea. He then told us it would probably be about an hour, but we could have the first band on by nine o' clock. Sounded okay to us lot, and we were to be the main band as well. He then said he would charge a fiver to enter the gig and this would go towards the beer and fags we had stolen. Well we couldn't argue with that, but if he only knew how much we had drunk and pinched, we would have had to play for a couple of weeks to repay him.

We were then waiting downstairs with all our friends for the all clear to go back up and start the gig. Other people had now started to come into the pub. It seemed by word of mouth and telephone the gig had now been properly advertised, albeit belatedly and it wouldn't be a massive crowd, but the locals from around the area, wanting to see live Punk music, would all turn up.

We were allowed back up the stairs about 7:30pm – just the bands that is – to set up. Because we'd been told by the controlling bodies that booked our gigs that everything would be there, we had only brought our guitars, a practice tuner amp, drumsticks and a couple of microphones. The other band was very similar, but they had forgotten microphones, so we would let them borrow ours. It didn't look promising, but I borrowed a bass amp and the sound engineer linked up a microphone to the practice amp which Gordon was to use, and pushed the sound through his PA. It looked a bit stupid, but what a sound, and luckily the pub had its own drum kit always there. Sorted. The gig was on.

The first band was to go on at 8:30, so the door at the bottom of the stairs was opened and the paying public came through. I was so happy to see Munchkin there; hadn't seen her for years and she was seeing the band for the first time. All went well. There were probably about ninety people there and totally enjoying themselves: Skins, Punks, Herberts and Bootyboys going mad, and the bar we had raided earlier had been refilled and manned, so everything now had to be paid for. By the time we got on and started playing, I must admit all four of us had had one or two pints over the top, but boy did we play fucking great that night – probably one of the best gigs we ever did – in the very front Munchkin and her party, and behind her was our lot going mental. It really was a good gig.

When it finally came to the finish like all gigs do, people started going or milling about by the bar for the last pint. Gordon and I started packing up our stuff; guitars in their cases, practice amp and guitar leads all gathered up, and Paul who had driven us was carting the stuff back to the van as we packed it, then the landlord came over.

"Who's got the money for the PA then?" he said.

Gordon and I looked at each other with surprise and, as usual in these circumstances, Gordon spoke:

"That bloke over there, mate," pointing to this Punk who had come in during the gig.

As the landlord turned round to see the the Punk he walked off into the toilet. Gordon and I turned round and made for the door as quickly as possible. As we went towards the exit, gathering all the bods that came with us, or sending others to retrieve all so we could get out fast, we moved outside towards the van and a bar staff member came out.

"Has the landlord seen you about money?" he said.

Everyone nodded their heads. "It's all sorted mate," Dan said.

We turned towards the van; also with us was Munchkin and her boyfriend as we had told them we would drop them back off in Stafford on the way home. It would give me time for a long chat on the way there, and we did have a long chat, didn't we Munch!!!?

I did feel sorry for the PA. bloke; he did a cracking job, but we didn't have the money to pay for this gig, and neither did the other band. We were stitched up from the start – no planning and sent off on nearly a wild goose chase. We did learn a lesson that night; every gig we played from then was arranged by us. God knows what the Punk did when the landlord got to him. It must have been funny – wish I could have been a fly on the wall then.

After we dropped off Munch and co, we headed off to Reading, stopping off again at a motorway service station; most were too drunk and asleep to do anything, but the odd couple did head towards a hidden spot for a bit of night time exercise out of the way of prying eyes.

We got back to Reading, dropping off people as we went through, and I didn't get home till at least 4 in the morning, knackered, still drunk but happy. More memories of a good gig and an old friend.

The Taser

As a skinhead you get to meet people and get asked to do things which the norms in the world just read about, it's just the nature of the beast to meet dodgy people and from these things you come out with toys to have fun thanks to one of these things we did for others. Dan and I came away with a couple of tasers for our own personal use (I'm not going to say who and where we got them but needless to say they were very hardcore criminals).

Dan and me sometimes used a local pub called the Carousel; it's not there any more, they pulled it down and put up some cheap housing (alleged) but filled it with scummy families who are just interested in drug selling and intake. Dan used the pub more than me and got to know a man in there called Bonk; he just happened to be a Dad of one of our good mates a skinhead (and still is D-Day, good old Andy, him and Julie his other half are salt of the Earth good friends). Anyway the two of us decided to go and have a pint or two during an afternoon session. As we walked in, there was Bonk sitting in his usual place on his own and two other blokes the other end of the bar. We just strolled over to Bonk, sat down with him and ordered our drinks.

Bonk was a professional drinker and it seemed not a lot of people sat with him or talked to him, but Dan and I got on like a house on fire with him and we had a laugh when we drank. On this day he didn't seem the same; he was a bit nervous and upset. The barman gave us our pints and Dan asked Bonk, "What's up, mate? You're quiet even for you."

He just looked at the two in the corner and nodded, "Those twats are taking the piss out of me, flicking peanuts every now and then."

"Well they won't do anything now, Bonk. We are here." Dan said.

We carried on drinking and chatting, but I could see by the look in Dan's eye that what Bonk told us had started his violent streak to take over all logic. The two at the other end of the bar didn't do anything else. We were there, but they were getting louder and with the odd look over to us.

Dan decided he needed a piss and got up and walked to the toilet. I kept my eye on him all the way. I knew what was going to happen; he looked at the two as he walked by. They looked at him and he gave them one of his impish smiles and a nod he went into the toilet.

I got up from the stool at the bar and Bonk looked at me. "Dan's on one," I said. "He is gonna do something." I put my hand in my MAI jacket and switched the Taser on, just in case. With Dan's temper and now a few beers, it had stewed in Dan's head someone picking on Bonk.

The door opened from the toilet and out came Dan. He had done up his jacket so it didn't flap everywhere and be grabbed easily. The two who had given Bonk trouble didn't know what was coming, nor could see Dan. The toilets were behind a wall that jutted out from the end of the bar, so you couldn't see who came out until they came round the wall. I could see; I'd waited away from the bar for Dan to come out. In one hand he had his police truncheon, in the other his taser. I could see the purpose in his eyes as he darted round the corner. Before the two could react, he had hit one on the head with the truncheon and the other the taser had made contact; you could hear the machine's electricity as he pushed the machine into the body. I saw the man just go stiff, shake and collapse to the floor. I had to make a move to help, but wasn't needed. The tasered man was out and pissing himself on the floor; the other who Dan had whacked was moving, starting to get up, bad mistake – ZAP – he was tasered. Same result: he pissed himself and was unconscious. By the time I got there it was over. We both knew it was time to move; the rumpus would surely bring the bartender through and some others from the other bar. Bonk had got up and had a massive grin on his face. The only words from him were an astonished, "FUCK ME". I just couldn't go, I had not used my taser. Zap! I got the first one again. I know it sounds cruel, but it just had to be done. It's a skinhead thing and a brother thing – you done yours, I'll do mine, so off we went to make a move to town and a few more beers.

All we found out was when the barmen and others came through, the bar was silent. Bonk was on his chair, drinking his Guinness, taking no notice of the carnage twenty feet from him. "Didn't see what happened, I was drinking."

Good old Bonk. Many didn't like him and he had his problems, but Dan and I did like him.

Slaying Monsters

All the real Skins every weekend would gather in the town centre. When I say *real* I mean the ones who showed their faces everywhere and not those who hid themselves in their own little streets to act hard in boots and a haircut but never joined the town's crew. Wannabees talked the talk, but never walked the walk, and our part of the town was the railway and bus station; all our local beer holes were around that part of town, easy to get to and to get home when drunk, not too far to stagger for a bus. We would get down town about 10 to 11ish and crew up. If I'd had German beer sent to me from my brother-in-law in Germany, I would take it down town and we would sit about the station and top up before we would go over to the station bar and get drunk — always a laugh and always entertainment.

On this particular day, a monster was to get a terrible kicking. We had as usual been sitting round the station having a beer, joking about, having a laugh and getting moved on every now and again from in front of the Gregg's café; we didn't give them trouble as we drank our teas there. It was just a laugh to have them come outside and say "Move on a tad, lads and girls, the customers are intimidated." So we would for an hour then go back, always the same, round by the station. Skins and some Punks would meet up, and we would have the usual gangs of girls {not Skins, possibly wanting to be one but not yet having the nerve} coming round and eyeing up us lot, and making contact with some of us. I loved watching our Wrens looking at them, trying to and in fact intimidating them if they got too close to a Skin they wanted. How our girls made friends I'll never know. They were tough girls, no shit and took no prisoners. Also round by the station you would get the down and outs, the town's dossers and druggies, or alcoholics. They would hang out in the subways that used to be round by the station, {they are all closed and boarded up now}. When we used to use the walkways to cut across the road or to go to our pubs, we would meet a few.

Every now and then you would smack a druggy. I hated them then and still do, or kick one of the dossers in the mouth. WTF – it's England, and this creature is squatting in the middle of a walkway hassling passers-by and dribbling or pissing himself. Oh no, SMACK – "NOW FUCK OFF!"

We sometimes got the coppers coming up to us and asking about certain dossers around the place. They had gotten info on some of them that were trying to intimidate young girls; they knew if we saw them the twats would move. An unofficial police deterrent we were.

We had come from the station bar; we'd had a good afternoon's bellyfull of beer and were in good mood. As we came up the steps from the underpass, we didn't notice behind us two dossers walking down the steps from the other entrance to the underpass keeping very quiet, heads down. As we got to the top there was a group of people round by a bus stop; they were chatting to two young girls, about twelve years old, who were crying. I recognised them as two young'uns that usually hung around with some girls that came round the station to chat to us; they were too young to go out with – probably sisters of some of the others, but they liked to be seen with the Skins.

As we came closer, one of the girls who was being comforted by some women and a bus driver, looked at me and, to my surprise, came over and grabbed me, and was crying. Her friend followed. There was Dan, me, D-day, I think, Sawyer and Simon. We were totally taken aback and the bus driver and the passers-by asked us if we were with them. We had to tell them they were just girls we saw every now and then.

I asked one of the girls, "What's wrong? Why are you crying?"

"That drunk man tried to take us — he touched us," one of them said.

At the same time this was being said, all you could hear was the bus driver and the passers-by that came to the girls' aid, all talking and pointing towards the twats who had tried it on with these young girls.

With all this going on, we realised who they were on about: the two that sneaked past behind us and were heading towards the station.

I suppose, with the aid of a bellyful of beer, we all went into kill mode; we ran over towards the station looking for the two perverts, couldn't see them; then just as we were about to go back, there they were in the station ticket room getting ready to go through to the trains. We went into the ticket office and made the decision there.

I walked over to the biggest one and smacked him straight in the face, shouting, "You pervert fucking monster!" Can't remember the exact words, but this was a cue for the others.

Like with a hungry pack of wolves these two twats were attacked; all we could see was red, and the thought of those two little girls. They were kicked all over the room, people screaming and shouting, running away. The ticket man just closed his box and hid; the ticket sellers pulled the shutters down and did the same. The two perverted monsters were by now getting a complete Doc Marten meeting — left right, left right; they were a mess, and by now the coppers were coming.

As we made an exit we looked to see if our buses were there: none. Oh fuck, but the gods were smiling; just as we were about to do a runner, Gosseburger stopped outside the station in his Mini {this lad was a tad rotund and I'd given him the name Grossburger as he looked like the lad from *National Lampoons Animal House*; he was a good Skin}. I don't know how, but we all got in his Mini. "DRIVE MATE, DRIVE! GO TO MY HOUSE!"

"What's up?" he asked.

"We just gave two of those druggy perverts a kicking. They're a fucking mess!"

"They tried it on and tried to take two little girls," Simon explained.

Grossburger got us away. Just as we left the station the police were arriving the other way. Thank fuck for Groosy; we would have been nicked, even though the police knew we patrolled this area.

We found out later that when the police questioned everyone, the bus driver told them what these two had tried, and that the Skins dealt him what everybody else wanted to do, and nobody gave them names or descriptions of us. Well that wouldn't have been hard: skinheads.

Also the two twats got arrested for trying to take the little girls; it was a while before they got out of hospital, but they then went to prison, where hopefully they got more kickings. A few years later, the big one I hit hung himself. Well there was no loss there. To tell the truth, if it wasn't for the fact we were in town and if it had been somewhere else, we would have hung the pair ourselves. They are not wanted on this planet; they are monsters, and should be put down, not treated for an illness. That's all I have to say on that matter.

The Aldermaston Raid

Just not too far outside Reading is the secret _Atomic Weapons_ _Establishment_ Aldermaston base, a place since the 50s till the present day that has made the hard water and electrical parts for Nuclear bombs; supposed to be a secret but, hey, THE WHOLE WORLD KNOWS.

With this base come the protesters, and all these bods camp outside the base in the woods. All sorts: Punks, hippies, CND, animal rights, anti this and anti that, just waiting for the next movement or cause to come along to go camp there and look a mess. They may have a point, but why look a mess 24-7? Also, I don't know why but there seem to be a lot of lesbian protesters there. I'm not bashing lesbians – it's everybody's right their sexual persuasion, but there are a lot, as we were to find out. Well, I did, up close and personal.

Dan, Simon, Paul and I had been drinking in a little pub not too far from the base and, after a bellyfull of beer and needing further entertainment, we decided to make a trip to the camp site. Staggering up the road towards the tents, we were all giggling, deciding what we were gonna do. The trip to the far end of the tents didn't take too long and we could only see shadows or an odd light if someone was walking through the tents, or from inside one. Dan's idea was to run through the site, pulling up as many tents as we could, making as much noise as possible and twatting anyone who tried to stop us. Great idea, if you were sober. Four pissed-up Skins wanting to do the charge of the light brigade isn't going to go without a few problems.

We all took deep breaths, chuckling and giggling; then went for it, shouting at the tops of our voices, screaming and swearing. We headed for the first tents, CRUNCH! All four of us straight over the top; made it, the first tents in tatters and bodies screaming and shouting, or in pain as our momentum had caused, but as you all know, if you're drunk and you run into something at speed, physics dictates that you lose all speed. It did and, as we picked our speed up again, we all seemed to pick different targets, but fortunately all the same direction. The other three seemed to have no trouble and continued to go on their merry way, causing mayhem and having the pleasure of twatting anyone in their path.

I, on the other hand, had trouble. I picked a target and ran at it. As I got near, I tripped and went head first through a partially-opened, zipped-up tent. Shock, horror; as I came crashing through I landed on my stomach in-between a girl's legs who was laid on her back, whose trousers were off and just in her knickers on her bottom half. On top of her was another girl sat astride her facing the laid-out girls face. She was just in her underwear, {*Maybe they were having a deep conversation?*}. The one on top looked around straight at me. The girl on her back moved her body and she looked at me too. All quiet except for the sounds of the turmoil going on around us outside.

Wallop! The one on top smacked me. Screams and shouts as they both tried to get to their feet and attack. "HELP, HELP – RAPE, RAPE!"

The one on top was shouting rape. Even drunk, I thought,What? I'm fucking pissed, can't run, I've come crashing through a tent, I hurt, I've landed in front of a bird with legs spread and in yellow knickers and another bird on top, and you're shouting rape? And to top it you are hitting me. Fuck it: self preservation mode kicked in. You hit me, I'll hit you {I'm not one of those peeps who think it's correct to hit ladies, but if they hit you first, fair's fair}. On my feet as fast as I could, punched the girl who hit me, and tried to get out of the tent. CRUNCH! The girl in her yellow knickers hit me with a hockey stick. Fuck –it hurt

– had to get out. When you think of it, must have looked funny from outside; all the light which was around would have shown three silhouetted bodies struggling, fists flying and a hockey stick being used as a weapon. On the reality side, I was fucking panicking: two very uptight girls, very angry, after my blood. Freedom: I got out. Fuck – where were the others? Just ran for the nearest gap. As some people will know, my eyesight is not the best, and when I was younger didn't wear my glasses outside and this night it didn't help being drunk. I ran for the gap – SPLOSH – straight into a dug-out bog. Fuck, it was going from bad to worse – a dug-out bog, in the middle of a camping site – a shit and piss hole. Fucking dirty hippy shites, I thought. I got out of the hole, stinking of hippy crap and made for the open road to where the others would have run.

As I came to the road I saw them all cracking up.

"What happened to you? We were just coming to find you," Dan said.

"What is that fucking smell – and what's that all on your boots and trousers?" Simon said.

"Fuck it, Spike! You're covered in shit. You got to get that off you," Dan said.

While all this was going on, we had moved off towards a garage. There we would use a phone and get a taxi home. Thankfully, Paul was loaded {a rare thing, a wealthy Skin}. As we got to the garage, we found a hose and, yep, I was washed down, my bottom half soaked AGAIN. How bad had it got, being laughed at by my brother and mates, being covered in shit and piss, been hurt falling over, attacked by two lesbians and now hosed down, wet, hurting, pissed-off, sobering up and maybe a ruined pair of boots.

The Christians

As I've said, I was in a band: a skinhead and Punk band and, in the early days of the band in Reading, we needed help, somewhere to practise and, if possible, some amps, speakers, et al to use, and hopefully not for a great deal of money. Luck by chance was on our side. Every now and then all the Skins and some Punks used to meet up down by the river, or any other park of our choice and play a game of footy or cricket, divide all in two and have a game. Great laugh, and we even followed the laws of both sports — well the blokes did, but the Wrens and even some of the Punks didn't have a clue. If it was footy, stick em in goal; if it's cricket the furthest boundary —out of sight out of mind. Anyway, we were all playing a game of footy, when I saw this bloke come over to our then first ever guitarist, (Pecker). I could see him having a chat, so while the others kept on kicking the shit out of each other under the guise of footy, Dan and I went to see what Pecker was up to.

When we got there he said, "This is my old music teacher, Mr Fenton. He is with all those over there."

Dan and I turned round to see about thirty men, women and children, totally inoffensive, all sitting round having a picnic or just kicking a footy between themselves.

"He wants to know if us lot fancy a game with them."

"What, footy?" I said.

"Yeah, eleven a side, but rolling subs."

I looked at Dan; he looked at me and we said okay. Then this Mr Fenton stuck out his hand and said, "Hello, I'm Dave Fenton. I used to teach Dave (Pecker) at school. I'm head of Music."

Dan and I just looked at each other – one of those Eureka moments. At the same time, this could be a productive meeting and game. (Harry: Mr Dave Fenton, later on did become a good friend of us, all Punks and Skins, a lot because of his extreme religious views and we all ended up calling him Harry, a nickname given to him by us, as there was a company in Reading called *Harry Fenton*, so we just called him Harry and it stuck).

As we walked back to the others, Pecker told us this lot all belonged to a Christian new Church. Dan and I just cracked up.

"You're having a laugh, Pecker. Fucking bunch of Christians want to play a gang of Skins and Punks at footy," I said.

"This is going to be carnage," Dan observed.

Pecker just did that funny little chuckle he did. If only we had known.

So we did get everyone ready. "We're gonna give a group of Christians a game, lads. Remember this is a game not a ruck."

All's well; both teams lined up. Well they did look good; all had footy boots on, or trainers, shorts, everything. We were in Doc Martens and any position on the pitch, like you do. All argued who was going in goal; no one wants to be the goalie. Why? The whistle was blown (they had a whistle and a ref; why didn't we see the signs?). Whoosh – they took the kick-off and within a couple of seconds – wallop: one up. Bloody hell, they are good and serious. We all stood about and had a laugh at the keeper (Ron I think), and then all realised we'd got to try. Okay lads, game head on it's Skin and Punk pride.

This time, after the whistle, we took it a little more seriously. Luckily, in the backs of our minds, we still knew how to play footy. In fact, some of us would probably have been pro's. But Punk and Skin came along and took over lives, and some of us were quite fit. I loved cycle-racing and raced, so I was fit-ish.

Anyway, the ball went out to the wing, Andy J. Off he goes; he could run, even with Doc Martens on. CRUNCH! One of the Christian defenders sent him flying through the air. The shock on his face and ours, and we thought it was gonna be a laugh. Well we did at poor Andy; he was just rolling in agony. It was funny and while we took notice of the game and tried to defend their attack, a lady had come over to Andy from the Christian party and asked him if he was okay. Typical Christian, kick the shit out of someone then give him love. What a different world.

Well that's the way the game went. We gave as hard as they dished out – bloody brilliant. Thank God we had rolling subs; we needed it.

Can't remember the score. We lost, but they did catch us off guard. The next time (and there were quite a few more) we would be ready; we even played a couple of games on the local secondary school field where Harry taught. A privilege that was; nobody got to do that except school sports, and to top that Harry would go on to help us. We even used the school where he taught for band practice, all their equipment and a studio. It was great and didn't cost a penny, just agreed to whatever game the Christians wanted. It looked good for their Church, playing sports with the town's local hoodlums in their local mag and we had a laugh playing them and got some munchies as well. You know what those Christians are like, feeding the five thousand et al.

I've often wondered whatever happened to Harry and their Church. I think they were all saving up to build an actual church, but like life is, things changed. We as a band moved on and lost contact with them all. We got very extreme and it wouldn't have been good for Harry and his friends being in contact with what we were saying and singing. He was a good bloke and a TRUE CHRISTIAN, as I understand it, but there you go, and I don't think we would have ever become a skinhead Christian band. What a thought!

Punks

As I've said before, I was a Punk for a time, thanks to my auntie. From late '75 until '77 I was one of those spiky-haired, pogo-dancing lunatics; it was fun for a time. It wasn't just the music that got me into it, but the look. IT HAD ITS OWN LOOK. That's why Punks stood out. Yep, a uniform: a new cult with a new uniform. I fucking hate it when people say it isn't. What's wrong with that word? Just because it's the word UNIFORM? That's what makes Punks et al: the clobber, not just the music. Could you imagine all those that say it's not the clothes you wear, but the inside that counts. Oh woopy-doo let's all dress like bankers and have nice posh haircuts, but still call ourselves Punks because we liked the *Sex Pistols*. Rubbish! The clothes go with it – that is what makes it exciting and different.

I had and still have loads of Punk mates. I love being around them and the Punk scene. I had many great times with them and the music from the 70s until about '91 was great, but things changed and I watched it happen. It lost its meaning and direction and, for a time, it nearly died.

Why did this happen? AMERICA. Every time those lot over there get their hands on one of our cults, they change it, they butcher it and the music goes to pot. Punks walking around with ¾ length trousers and trainers, with a fucking skateboard. Oh please do me a favour – fuck off! You've just got to look at their Punk bands of the 90s. What they were going on about in their songs? Who wants to know about the political scene in the States? Who fucking cares? I don't know what happened to the Yanks back in the 70s and early 80s; bands like

130

Ramones, *Dickies*, and *Patti Smith* were great, but they lost something, and then the late 80s and 90s came and yet again the clothes. Fuck me – a pair of trainers a couple of stains on their jeans or ¾ length army surplus a pin somewhere on the jumper or jacket and a haircut a priest would be proud of. But have one member of the band with a non-brushed style and maybe, and I say maybe, a tad splodge of colour slapped on somewhere in the hair, then the music. Lets make it poppy and funny, so we can have it on the radio, maybe an odd swear word thrown in for shock value every now and then. AND YET AGAIN THEY PUT RAP INTO IT SOMEWHERE.

Yep, you probably guessed I think the Yanks nearly killed Punk and other cults to boot, just look what they did for Skins: ¾ length trousers again, a goatee and a bald head and must be a Nazi. What a load of wankers! Fuck knows what they will do to Mod culture. Probably the same in clothes and those fucking trousers again and put mirrors on a skate board or surf board. Punks in parka's – what the fuck is that about?

Another thing that gets on my nerves is when a group is classed as POST Punk. What the feck is that? Just because the band is older, or it's not 1977, doesn't make them not Punk; you are or aren't a Punk band. Post Punk – what a crappy saying. I don't know; maybe I'm old... NO, I KNOW HOW THE CULTS SHOULD BE. THEY ARE AN ENGLISH CREATION AND WE KNOW HOW TO LOOK GOOD AND CREATE NEW MUSIC.

I'm glad to say, from the ashes of the fire going out, the Brits have taken it back. Punk is still alive and kicking, although I must say some of the songs sound a tad like the grungy thrash shite, but at least they look like Punks and the music has found what it was in the beginning: fast aggressive heart-pounding, with a word to say or two. All I want from Punks is to be Punk: the clothes, the hair, the colours – all of it. Who gives a fuck what the liberal-minded, uni-educated twats think who say it's the feeling inside, not the clothes. Bollocks! Punk is Punk, is Punk...

France

I've been to France five times: once with the school and once with the band, and that stays in my mind for another time. Once to Dieppe for a stag do: very drunk, but I liked the place. But the other two times I'll tell about now, and how different but entertaining they both were.

One Friday Morning my missus tells me I've been asked if I want to go to France with my brother-in-law {he was a European coach driver}. A long weekend it would be: get there Friday evening and return on Monday. Yeah, I thought, sounds good. Never been to Paris; some beers, try and make contact with the locals (girls) and have a laugh.

I was picked up by my brother-in-law and taken to the coach park where I put my holdall of clothes in with his in the driver's own personal part of the coach, but kept my supplies with me: BEER, LOTS OF BEER. Nothing special; we drove around picking up people for the trip – all around the Aldershot area and headed for the coast. God knows what the people thought. It was '81 or '82, height of the skinhead-bashing press era. We were all Nazis and thugs and most of the general public believed that: another press victory controlled by our marvellous government of the time. Strange looks as they all got onto the coach. I had the single seat at the front of the coach, boots up on the rail in front and a can of ale to boot. Most of the passengers were old, and as they got on they just looked and then shut up. I could hear the whispers as they went by and, from the corner of my eye, see the pointing. What a laugh, and chatting to the driver.

The trip to the coast was uneventful. I thought to myself, take it easy on the beer, don't want to get ranted before I even get on the ship, but thankfully re-supply. As always, customs was the same anywhere in England; the only person who was stopped and given the third degree was the skinhead in the coach party: ME.

"Where you going, how long for, who with? "They didn't believe I was with the driver. All my stuff was taken from the coach, searched for propaganda (this twat said), or controlled substances the French don't want you taking over there. *Oh thank you, I'm not only a Nazi thug, but drug pusher as well.*

Half-an-hour later, I was let on the ship and rejoined the coach party, my brother-in-law chuckling away.

"You did say that would happen," he said.

"Fuck off and let's get to the duty free – need some more beer," I replied, all the time looking at the faces of some of the coach party. They were disgusted to see I was free to travel. The boat trip was fine, all re-supplied and a little nap on the way over; even when we disembarked I had no hassle from the French customs come to think of it. Our coach was just waved through, the brother-in-law just had to get out and have his paperwork checked at the border checkpoint. The trip across France was great. I love the country; it just seems to flow with a course at the end, but always a feeling that the French people don't take shite from their government and they let them know that.

We got to Paris. Oh my God – what a shock. History, I love it, the feeling of the city, love it, but traffic? I don't think there is any planning at all, and traffic lights are just a suggestion and not a means of control. You have to be brave to drive there. Thank fuck we were in a coach; even that didn't stop some of the locals driving around cutting us up. Thankfully I was the only one who could hear Dave (the brother-in-law – God rest his soul) swearing and cursing the driving style of the Parisians, but we pushed our way through. We were heading for the Avenue des Champs Elysees. Our hotel wasn't far off that, but this road is a mile long, wonderfully full of shops, cafés, drinking holes, everything fantastic both sides of the road, but it's the same thing:

loads of coaches going the same way with the traffic fighting its way through from one end to the other. This is where I had my first meeting with a local who I'd see later.

Halfway up the road we had to pull over a bit and stop – don't know the reason why, we just did. The coach door was open to let in some air. Dave said it was getting stuffy and coaches back then, even posh ones, weren't as good as nowadays, and a door open meant cool air coming in. As we were waiting to go, I saw a squat Turkish-looking bloke standing just outside the open door of the coach and looking at me. I'd had a few beers, so I just looked back at him. I looked at Dave and could see a bit of nervousness. I stood up and, in my most brilliant English, I said, "What's up mate – what's wrong?"

A big grin comes on his face and he says in a very strong French accent in English, "'OOLIGAN, YOU 'OOLIGAN FOOTBALL, YOU 'OOLIGAN?"

Well that caught me off guard. What do you say to that? Had to think quick.

"Fucking right I am, Chelsea Hooligan."

The bloke just smiles and says, "You have English beer? English beer good – give you two for one."

Again that caught me off guard. Did he really say two for one? I just looked at him.

"Give you three for one."

"Yeah, okay," I said. I had ten cans left and if this went okay I'd get thirty for them. Don't matter what it's like; it's beer and thirty is better than ten. As I'd been in conversation with this local, all the passengers were looking on wide-eyed and open-mouthed. There they were, wanting to get to the hotel; we're in a traffic jam and I'm doing business at the open door with a local, who I discovered was a doorman in a local drinking establishment. All went well; he gave me the beer which he had already stacked and I gave him my tins of Courage lager. He must have done this many times before, and the beer he gave me was well in date and 4%. We shook hands and he called me a 'ooligan again and, before I had any more chance to learn French, we moved off, a big smile on my face and more beer to keep me going now.

It didn't take long to get to the hotel and all I can say, it was PLUSH. Booking in was a great laugh (*tres amusant*): a coach load of oldies and snobs and I walk in, boots, braces and a swagger. I was to stay in the room with the brother-in-law. We got settled, put our little bit of luggage away and got freshened up. A nice shower, a bit of a shave and polished the boots.

We were going to go out and have a beer, and I had a destination in mind. We left the hotel about 7pm. I asked Dave, who knew the district, to take us back down where we had seen the doorman who had swapped his beer for mine. We got to the strip and walked around for a bit looking for somewhere to have a drink. I really did stand out: black Harrington, a nice Brutus shirt, my burgundy braces, Wrangler jeans with a half-inch turn-up and my ox blood fourteen hole DM's. Great, felt good. Problem being not a lot of people knew there was tension from different ethnic groups in Paris.

We were warned not go off the main streets, but I wanted a drink and the obvious places were the back streets where *real* people are and not the hordes of tourists and play-acting Parisians acting up for them. We walked in the back streets for about five minutes and, lo and behold, the doorman we'd met was in front of us. As he turned round he smiled and came up.

"'ooligan, hello, you come with me for beer, good place many friends."

Well, why not – what could happen, a kicking? I hoped not, though I've had many. It was Dave I was thinking of, but it all just seemed okay, so off we went to this bar. As we walked in, all the locals turned round and stared; a skinhead had walked into a bar full of Turkish-looking French with one of their own. It was an oops moment. Had I (we) made the wrong turn? No problem, our new friend (Joel his name was) introduced us to the owner and barman of the pub and he told his friends it was me, the Hooligan, who had swapped beer with him. It broke the ice and a beer was had. Although I couldn't understand a word that went on, Dave could, and he kept an ear out.

Anyway, as the time went on I found out this was a district for Algerians and they were having some trouble with new immigrants that had moved into the area from Mali. This was way above my head: French speaking Algerians and French speaking Malians having fisticuffs. All this I was trying to take in, standing at the bar drinking, listening to broken English and the odd translation from Dave, then the shit happened. Out of the corner of my eye I saw a group of African people outside the front of the pub. As they walked in I saw our new friend Joel and two others walk over to the group. I knew straightaway; maybe after years of being in Skin and pub fights you got to know when trouble was imminent. I grabbed Dave and pulled him over to the far wall. He just looked at me, puzzled.

"Watch this Dave and keep your head down. It's gonna go off."

As the three doormen got to the Africans, the group just attacked and more came in with bats. Wow, a real bar fight. I'm not involved and it looks nasty. I'm only here for sight-seeing and beer. Now I've got my brother-in-law in deep shit – oops. As the fight escalated more of the locals in the bar joined in – lots of different languages being screamed and glasses or chairs being thrown. It was like watching a film, but nothing came our way and we just stood and watched these two groups going at it.

"Fucking hell, Spike, we've got to get away," Dave said.

"I ain't walking that way yet mate. I'm sure to get a beating and probably you too; the Bill has to be here soon."

And like good old Blighty, within a few minutes they got there, and in Paris they don't fuck about – all in black combat gear and guns, body armour and shields, they jumped out of their vans and laid into the two groups. It didn't take long for the trouble to stop and the special version of the French SPG HAD WON THE BATTLE AND NICKED LOADS. Oh dear, they came towards us. Fuck, they were walking towards me, I was in trouble.

About three feet away the barman came to our aid. He explained we were tourists (me a tourist?) and were just having a beer when the trouble started – total innocence. Then this massive French copper in front of me, looking like *Robocop*, in an English voice said, "We don't get many English skinheads in this part of the city. I suggest you get back on the main street, it's safer, especially for you," as he pointed at me.

Well you didn't have to tell Dave and me twice, not just back to the main street, back to the hotel we scarpered. Needless to say, no more out-of-the-way pubs for the weekend.

The rest of that evening went okay. We got back to the hotel; Dave only had a couple of lemonades as he was driving again in the morning for more sight-seeing. I, on the other hand, wanted to test the assumption that the bars stayed open until the last person left. I ended up drinking by the bar with an American lady (very nice) until I was the only person left. I had some of my clothes given back to me in the morning at breakfast. It seems I got that drunk, I was undressing to go to bed as I walked to the lift. I don't remember getting to bed; one of the hotel staff got me to my room, but they didn't want to upset me. Nice people; God knows what happened to the Yank lady, who knows?

Well the rest of the weekend went relatively uneventful, except I did get lost round by the parliamentary buildings not far from the Eiffel Tower and, once again, a van load of black-clad armoured cops with guns jumped out at me. It's amazing how polite you get when confronted with automatic guns. Then again, I now know how people felt when they bumped into me with automatic weapons while serving in the armed forces. They accepted my excuse that I was lost and pointed me back to the tourist-friendly zones, which I was glad to get to. If I had been nicked here on a weekend's jolly, the missus would have crucified me. Anyway, from that moment on I kept with the coach party. No more walkabouts or back street bars – just sight-seeing and beer. All harmless stuff.

Channel Crossing

The second skinhead trip to France was rather more clandestine and dangerous.

During the mid to late 80s, Reading had a big skinhead following and with this came Skins from Europe. In Reading we had two Germans and two Frenchmen; one of the French lads I'll call Paul, just in case he is still wanted. Now Paul was a bit of a lad; he was always in trouble, and it had caught up with him. Paul had a very nasty past, especially with the far right. He was really proud of his grandfather who had served with Leon Degrelle and the Wallon 28 SS Wallonien Division during World War 2, and he always carried a picture. Well, it takes all sorts to make a world. Paul had gotten in trouble and had beaten up a lefty student; he already had a case pending and with this he would have got a prison sentence, so with this assault on top, it should have been bye-bye Paul for some time, but fate had a plan.

Paul had come round to our house to see Dan and me, and moan and whinge about the upcoming court case and probable incarceration. He wanted to do a runner; he had missed his pending court case and a warrant was out for his arrest. He wanted to go back to France so what could we do? He couldn't now use any port or airport, not with a warrant out. Dan and I had done some stupid things in the past and even got away with them, but human smuggling was a new criminal enterprise.

Stage enter right: Gav and Waistcoat arrived at the house. These two were a lot younger, but phenomenal rogues, especially Gav; he was into everything. Drugs (which, as you know, I don't like), theft, cars, houses, warehouses, anything, and we had not seen either of them for ages, but they turned up and Mum made tea as we caught up. Then, as we were chatting, Gav comes out with a stunner. He had got involved with a posh bird, and her father had a little boat and had paid for Gav to train to get his boat navigation and captain's licence. As he told us this, Dan and I just looked at each other, had the same idea and smiled.

"You got a boat licence, you can navigate — what for rivers and that, or sea?" Dan asked.

"Both, it's a great laugh. Waistcoat and me have had loads of over the water trips."

Gav said this with a smile, meaning it was bound to be illegal.

Well, the conversation went only one way from then. Gav and co were updated on what was going on with Paul and what he wanted to do. They were straightaway into the idea, which we planned there in the kitchen of our house with Paul looking on, picking up the odd word. His English was okay, but when you get four Skins planning an invasion of France in a little boat, I think some words just went right over his head. To cut a long story short, we had a plan: that weekend we would go down to where the boat was moored: Littlehampton, and then the great adventure would take place. Looking back now, we could have got into real trouble, or gone down for a long stretch, but at the time this was an adventure, a laugh and just helping out a mate, even if he was a mental Frenchman, but this turned out to be one of the scariest trips and most stupid things we ever did.

Dan, Paul and I travelled down to Littlehampton. We got there about 10am. No one else knew what we were up to — just us five. Even Paul's girlfriend didn't know the plan, the fewer who knew the better. We met up with Gav and Waistcoat and they took us down to where the boat was. Shock horror! We thought it would be the size of a rowing boat, but this thing was something like the boat from *Jaws*.

"Fuck me, mate, you didn't say it was this big," I said.

"It's an old fishing trip boat, birds. Dad used to run it, it's got all the gear still," Gav said.

"We ain't going fishing with you two, we are smuggling Paul into France. You sure this will do it and you can get there?" Dan said.

Nod of the head and Gav and Waistcoat just smiled and chuckled with reassuring comments like, "Don't worry, done it before," but to tell the truth I was shitting it.

Gav told us he had informed the authorities he was taking the boat out and was doing a fishing trip. We didn't know he had to do this. What the fuck do we know about sea travel and boat stuff? The only experience Dan and I had with boats was using them in '78 to get into the festival and using a boat on the Thames to do Viking raids up and down the canals (a story for another time), but you have to inform the coast guard and authorities if you are in sea lanes, like you do when flying, but again we didn't know that and Gav had obviously done his stuff.

"We're fishing, well, they think we are," he told us all.

We got on the boat and looked around it. At least we couldn't see any water on the deck or in the galley. Then we saw what Gav and Waistcoat were dressed in: big fucking warm sea-going coats, bobble hats and welly type boots.

"What the fuck you two wearing?" Dan asked.

"Stuff to keep us warm going over, sea-going clothes," Waistcoat said.

"You didn't tell us. We're in our boots, braces and MA1 coats. If it's that cold we're gonna freeze and the boots will get ruined. Cheers Gav," Dan said.

"I thought you might have known; it is a boat, mate, going out to sea, sorry Dan," Gav said.

Oh well, we just followed Gav to where he controlled the boat and sat and watched as Waistcoat undid the ropes to the dock and came up to where we were. The boat had all the gear: radios for communication and a radar. This now took our attention, on top of the words spoken by Gav.

"Got to keep a good view on that for other boats and ships."

The thing is, when we all go to the seaside, all we see is the bit of the sea we are in and probably a few little boats bobbing up and down, and you take no notice, but when you're on a boat, that just seems to get smaller with all the traffic and, yes, traffic on the sea, it's an eye-opener: boats and ships of all sizes and speed. Now Dan and I aren't stupid when it comes to radars and radios. We were both in the armed services and used a lot of equipment, but to see so many dots on the radar and, by now, the sea was getting a tad choppy made us a little uncomfortable and, to top that, Waistcoat was put on a viewing platform to keep an extra eye out. Paul, by now was hanging his head over the side of the boat; he did not have sea legs. In fact, we probably had moved only a 100 yards before he was getting ill, and every minute we travelled the sea got choppier, and it had started to rain. Gone went the nice morning when we had arrived, and we wondered how much sick Paul could throw over the boat. Poor bloke, a real land-lubber.

While we left Paul to do his bodily functions over the side of the boat, Dan and I had found the beer. Well, it was gonna be a few hours on the boat and it was also a jolly as well as a smuggling trip. That's when Gav asked the question, "You did remember to bring your passports, didn't you?"

Dan and I looked at each other.

"No. Why, you joking?" I asked.

"In case a coastguard boat comes alongside, or we get asked at the dock where we are going," Gav said.

"You didn't say bring a passport, Gav. We aren't sight-seeing – we are getting Paul out of the country for fuck's. sake. What else you gonna surprise us with?" Dan said.

"It's just in case. I've got a plan anyway. We won't go to the port and dock. I know a little place," Gav said.

Well, that put a stop to our drinking. All fun went out the window;

now we had to worry about police, coastguard, border guards, probably interplod, and plus the weather wasn't very good and we were in the hands of Gav and Waistcoat, who were not known for their ideas coming off 100%. Oops, had we made a mistake?

Gav's plan was to head for Dieppe; then he said he would make a little detour to where he knew a little inlet where he made his business trips with Waistcoat, drop Paul off and head back to Blighty, if all went to plan. If not, we would be spending the next few days in a French prison cell waiting a smuggling charge, most likely extradition to England and a big fine, or probably prison time.

Dan and I then spent most of the trip chatting, trying to chat to Paul between sick times and hoping our two super smugglers did really know what they were doing. It was cold and we couldn't believe how many other boats and big ships were out in the sea lanes, and those big ships move fast when you get close, and our boat which we thought was big was getting smaller and smaller, and when the bigger ones went by the wake knocked the boat up and down and side to side, Dan and I just laughed, but I think Paul was close to death by now; all he did was moan and swear in French. Yeah, he knew we were helping him, but he hated the sea and boats. Gav shouted for Dan and I to go to the bridge.

"Change of plan, mate, we're going straight into Dieppe, too much traffic today to go around and find the inlet we use. Done it before, don't worry."

Dan and I were past worrying by now; all we needed was dry land to get Paul off and go home without incident. Now the port of Dieppe has changed a lot. Now it has a massive modern dock where the passenger ships dock a far distance away from the fishing and pleasure boats. Back in the 80s the big boats docked not too far away from the fishing and pleasure fleet, so loads of traffic came in and out. Luckily, the immigration and border police were not as good or visible as they are today and, unbeknown to us, the boat of ours had a good French name. We had not even noticed it: BONNE DE LA FRANCE. That's why every time they came to the French coast they were not challenged. Think about it: French name. French boat, French crew.

We came into the port at a good steady speed. Yep, Gav did know what he was doing; he and Waistcoat were even waving at some of the locals on their boats as we came in. Paul, by now, had a massive smile on his face and was shouting hello's to other boats, brilliant. A Frenchman on a French boat chatting to locals. Dan and I, we just sat and watched.

"Bloody hell, Dan, we got here. No Titanic situation and Gav and co actually know what they are doing."

"Yeah, Spike, at the moment. You know their history. Someone's bound to recognise them or have an issue with them. Let's wait till we are back out to sea."

Wise words from my brother. Fingers were crossed.

Gav slowly brought the boat to a mooring place, a bit of distance from the next little fishing boat. Waistcoat jumped off and tied the boat to a massive bit of wood, and then we all stood and waited as Paul got his gear together and came over to us all. He shook hands with Gav and Waistcoat, said his thank you and turned to Dan and I. In his brilliant French accent he said in English, "I'll never forget you two, you helped me. I'll try and contact you, or I'll get Donna (his girl friend) to give you a message." With that he gave us a handshake and hug each (thank fuck not one of those French man kisses on the cheek).

"What's your plan then, Paul?" I asked.

"I'll catch a train or something back to Leon (where he was from) and take it from there."

"Well, mate, all the luck to you. Don't do anything stupid, well too stupid, and maybe we will see each other soon, and remember the band has its first French tour soon. Maybe see you then," Dan said. With that, Paul turned, bag over his shoulder and walked off, chatting to a few local fisherman as he went. There weren't many Skins in this part of France and he stood out.

We didn't get to see him ever again. The tour we were supposed to do never came off. Dan and I were arrested for guns; the drummer (another one) was sacked for drugs and the people we were supposed to be linked with and had done the gigs for stitched us up. Fucking politics: lesson well learned. We found out Paul went from Leon to Paris, got in trouble again, but then joined the Foreign Legion. He was lost into that lot of psycho's and probably loved it. How long he did, or what he did, we don't know. If he is alive I'd love to see him now. For all his political obsession he was a good bloke and, like I always did, I saw the man and not the act or political view. That's what counts. Gav and Waistcoat in the end drifted away from the skinhead scene, went their own way. The last time I saw Waistcoat he was a tipper lorry driver and doing well. Gav, I understand was still with a rich girl. Were they both straight? I don't know, but I doubt it – true real life Fagins they were.

The Funeral Punch-Up

Some strange events in your life stay in your memory forever, and some of these events happen just out of the blue, unexpectedly, when you should not even have been involved. This is what happened to us in 1993.

Dan, me, Ron Edge, Taff (who wasn't a Welshman but a Yarpi {South African}, but his last name was Jones so we called him Taff), Bristol Dave and a Skin we had just recently met called Raymond (Raygun) who always had ideas to make money, but they always went tits up. Dan and Raygun had had an idea to go and buy a load of Army surplus in bulk and we would sell it and make a mint. So Dan, Ray and I put in a lot of money and the others just wanted to come along and possibly buy some stuff cheap, or pinch something.

Ray didn't drink; he had some sort of allergy to alcohol, so he would drive us in an old Army Jeep he had. The place we were going was somewhere near Salisbury can't remember exactly where, but a big warehouse. So all six of us piled into this old Jeep on a Friday morning and set off. It looked pretty good; we had a little trailer in tow and we were all in good moods and had a fair bit of money.

We didn't stop; just drove straight to the place we had to get to. Just outside the estate, there was a pub, quite big with a church opposite. We decided to stop there and check it out for some food and a quick beer before going to the warehouse. Nice place, pretty big inside with a room set aside for parties or probably just to eat, with lots of tables all done up nice. There was a smaller room with more tables, both rooms with a bar, and then just a normal average third bar, probably where all the locals would have their beer, but nobody in there at this time.

It had just opened and we were the only ones in, but the people running it said yep to our food orders: plenty of eggs, bacon and sausages with lots of toast, sorted.

As we were eating we started talking to one of the girls who worked there, the usual things being said, "We don't get a lot of skinheads around here and none come in here, so you lot are being watched".

We didn't mind, being used to that, and we weren't out for trouble. Dan, Ray and I were going to do some business, the others, well they were after what they could get at the warehouse, by any means.

Ron went up to the bar to get some beer. When he came back with his tray of five pints and a coke, he told us, "There is gonna be a funeral over there," as he pointed to the church. "Then the wake is gonna be in those other two rooms; they reckon there is gonna be loads of bods coming."

Well that explained all the posh tables and chairs in the other rooms. Just as we were leaving, Taff asked if it would be okay if we came back later. The Landlord said yeah, it was okay, but the place would be full and we might not be able to get food. He also said he wasn't looking forward to the afternoon. It seemed the family of the dead man were all at war with each other (over money we later found out) and they were always knocking the shit out of the oppo's. Well that was their problem, not ours.

We got to the warehouse which was fantastic. All it did was kit for Army surplus; it was like being kitted out when I joined the forces.

Strange looks from the owners as a load of Skins got out of the Jeep. We didn't think all of us would be allowed in but, to our surprise and delight, we all signed in and off we went. Dan, Ray and I went round with one of the owners. His face started to light up as we went round picking not just an odd item but bulk buys. The others split up and went looking for what they wanted. Ohhh dear; they should have been supervised.

After about an hour's worth of going round the warehouse, we had finished. We were at the checkout getting all our bought items put into boxes for us to load on our trailer. Good days. Then we looked about for the other three. Ron and Taff came up together with just a couple of pairs of Army strides (trousers) and a pair of boots. No sign of Bristol Dave.

"Got what you want boys?" Dan said.

Big smiles on their faces and nodding of the heads.

"Where is Dave?" I said.

"He got fed-up and bored not having any money and following us around," Taff said.

Dan and I just looked at each other. Dave didn't get fed-up and bored; he would look for something to nick or do he was a natural comedian. Well, there was only one place he could have gone, unless he had been nicked – the Jeep.

So as we all walked away to put the boxes in the trailer, "Where's the Jeep? Someone has fucking nicked the Jeep!"

Panic hit all our faces. Then from our right the Jeep slowly came up with Dave driving.

"How the fuck has he got the keys to the Jeep?" Ray said, looking at me.

"I gave them to Ron in case we dropped them whilst walking round," I said.

"Dave wanted to sit in the van, Spike. He didn't say he was driving around." Ron looked sorry and concerned.

We all looked at each other, swearing at Dave as he slowly pulled up. Just as Ray was going to give him shit, Dave said, "Just get the fucking stuff in quick and don't let those blokes see in the Jeep!"

Ray shut-up quick as he caught on straightaway. We all looked at each other and started smirking as we loaded the trailer. Dan went over to the Jeep and started talking to Dave, both had impish grins on their faces. It didn't take long to load the trailer, then we got in the Jeep. Dan, Ray and I were okay, as we got in the front, but when Taff and

Ron tried to get in the back the floor was filled with kit. Dave, whilst walking round, had cased the joint. He'd then got the keys, moved the van round the side of the warehouse where he had seen a fire door with kit stacked in front of it. He'd pushed the door ajar a little and, when he drove the Jeep up to the side, he just stacked as much as he could in and under the seats. Trousers, jackets and some boots. Fuck it, we had to get out quick, and as we pulled away we were all laughing our heads off. What a result.

We made our way back to the pub, for something to eat and we now wanted a proper beer. Ray would be sober, so all would be well, so we thought.

When we got back to the pub the other two rooms were beginning to fill up with all the bods that had gone to the funeral. We walked up to the drinking bar and were recognised by one of the girls. She gave us a smile and said the obvious, "Oh you're back."

We all smiled, got our beers and even had some sandwiches made. We then got a table and made merry. While we were sitting, Ray was bartering with Dave about the gear he'd nicked. He had got at least five hundred pounds worth of stuff and Dave offered him two hundred and fifty for it, plus he could keep a pair of boots, a MA1 jacket and a pair of strides. Dave thought about it over a few beers, which Ray got him to soften him up and then they shook on it.

By this time we had all, except Ray, had a few. This meant some music was in order, and Ron was filling the jukebox up with money. But NO MUSIC. At the bar, he was asking why his music was not coming on.

"Because of the funeral party they might moan," he was told.

Ron then said, "I don't want it loud, just so we can hear it."

The bar staff then relented and switched all the other speakers off, and so we had music, thanks to Ron, although most of it was shit if you can remember the charts of the 80s and 90s. Then again, all the Smoovies and Smellies would disagree.

The afternoon went great. We got steadily pissed and all talked about the money we were going to make, and Dave the money he had already made.

Then it happened: the funeral wake exploded as the two sets of families started arguing; the alcohol they had consumed had now ignited their hate for each other. It didn't matter about the bloke who died; it now became an argument about money. We could see the bar staff and the landlord go over to try and make peace, or to say enough is enough and time to leave.

We thought it was funny and had gone and stood by the open doorway to the function room to watch. Then a woman from one of the groups just threw a glass across the room at a man. It went crazy: about twenty people just ran at each other and started shouting, screaming, pushing, shoving and fighting. The bar staff ran; the landlord was somehow on his back as someone had clocked him and knocked him out. We were over the moon just watching, laughing and egging on. Well you had to; it was just mental, and we had not started anything. Then as one of the women who was pissed up walked past, she said,

"What you lot laughing at? Fuck off!"

Well it had to happen. I suppose the beer and being ranted at was the trigger.

"You fuck off, you ugly warthog!" Taff said.

She swung at him, swearing. He just pushed her away and she fell backwards, too drunk to walk properly, but as she fell she screamed. All we saw then was a bunch of blokes and women coming at us. Here we go, I thought. A beer glass went straight over all our heads, showering us in beer and that was IT.

Without hesitation we all threw our glasses and these hit the charging lot. More swearing. There was only one thing to do, or get a hiding; we charged. Dan went first; he had a stool in his hand – smash! Got this woman and bloke. The charging mass hesitated and we were on them straightaway, all throwing punches and hitting anything we could. Then to our utmost horror, the others who had been arguing and fighting this lot started throwing glasses and bottles at *us*. FUCKERS. We were now being attacked by the ones who had been getting a kicking.

I suppose it was a classic case of the enemy of our enemies. We were now being attacked on two sides: glasses and bottles bouncing off us, ducking punches, but we were holding our own. We had to move backwards to the exit and get out of this tight arena, or we could have gotten caught and then maybe more than a kicking. As we moved to the door, Dave grabbed some pool cues and we took a stand outside.

A quick look at each other and I saw damage on all of us. Ron and Ray had blood gushing out of head wounds from bottles or glass; they would need stitching. I had a lump coming up the size of an egg on the side of my cheek I'd been hit with something and it had done its work. As we stood waiting for them to come out, we heard that familiar sound that always follows a ruck.

"Fuck it, the plod," Dan said. But we couldn't go anywhere; we had to go through the pub to the other exit to get to the Jeep that was parked on that side of the pub, and the plod had come from all directions.

As usual they steamed us. There we were, covered in blood, battered and bruised and had pool cues in hand. How guilty can you look? It must have been Christmas and birthday for the Bill when they turned up and saw us. We were all nicked and thrown into a paddy wagon (police van). Fucking brilliant! We'd been having a good time, someone else starts a ruck and we get nicked.

As we were all sitting in the back of the van, other meat wagons (police vans) turned up, as did ambulances. In the back of the van we were giving the plod verbal; we had been attacked; we had defended ourselves; they were the ones all knocking the shit out of each other. But the plod just looked at us and said the usual "You're still singing the same old song". Probably, yeah, but we were fucking stitched up on this occasion.

After a while the coppers realised we needed to be looked at by paramedics. We were all bleeding and looked a mess, and Ron and Ray had lost loads of blood. Their shirts were soaked by now. So we were taken out of the van, still handcuffed, and taken over to a waiting paramedic. As he looked us over and told the Bill we all needed to go to hospital, some of the bar staff were now talking to the plod. Then a sergeant came over with the girl we had been chatting to all day.

"You lucky sods, you lot are off the hook," he said.

We all looked at each other, surprised but happy.

"This young lady has told us what happened. Those lot are the trouble makers and you lot were caught up in it."

As our cuffs were taken off, we said thanks to the girl. She then told us the landlord had taken a bad kicking and was off to hospital. The funeral party were of two different gypsy families and no one else would let them have the wake at their premises. Everyone knew there would be trouble at some time, but no one knew a bunch of Skins would be at the pub on the same day.

Looking back, we were lucky. Stitches, cuts and bruises we had and ached for a while, and a load of pikies got nicked. That makes a change. We never, ever went back to that pub, never found out how bad the landlord had been hurt, and also that young pretty bar staff she had a great pair of legs and arse, and eyes to die for.

Our making money enterprise went sour. All the stuff was at our house, and during a night-time raid by the plod, everything was taken. They thought we had nicked them and we didn't have the receipts. Ray did, and he had done a bunk after he had problems with his missus.

Not long after, Ron moved back to Cornwall – lucky bastard – one of the loveliest parts of this planet. Bristol Dave went back to Bristol; he stopped being Skin after a kicking he got, ironically from gypsies of Bristol. Taff? We didn't have a clue what happened to him. He knew I was a Wiccan, and he got into it some; then he went completely over the top and joined the New Age Travellers. From Skin to hippy; at least if they get any trouble that's one hippy who can handle himself.

Mr West and the Crombie

I've previously said in this book about the first time I saw a burgundy Crombie coat, so here is the tale.

I'd bought a brand new bowler hat. A few of us liked to dress like *Clockwork Orange*, and sometimes at night we would patrol the underground subways in Reading (before they closed them). Then when we went into the pub it turned heads.

I was trying on the hat when the doorbell went ding dong. Mum shouted up that there was someone to see me. I left the hat on and came downstairs, seeing a pretty young Mod girl who was a friend I'd known since a kid, and someone I'd not seen for a while, even though she was a friend of my sister and went to school with her. She was called Linda. A big smile came to my face on seeing her, and I came down to give her a hug, before noticing that she was with a fresh-faced young Mod bloke, her boyfriend.

She returned the hug and said, "This is Ian, my boyfriend."

I looked at him; he seemed a tad nervous. I shook his hand – a Mod in the Pitt brothers' household – but I liked him straightaway; he just had something about him and also he had on this brilliant looking burgundy Crombie. It was fantastic. Dan and I had just had Crombies made for each other in the standard black, but with velvet collars and pockets – nice, but this coat looked great.

Anyway, we got talking. I had to ask Linda how things were, say that it was great to see her, this and that – yadda yadda, but my eyes kept looking at that *lush* coat, and I think what made young Ian more nervous was the fact I still had blood on my face. I had to explain that the night before, coming home from the pub, I'd been ambushed by some black lads, who'd jumped out of a car and just attacked me. I then put my back up against a tree and, with my walking stick, which I carried at night, had tried to defend myself as best I could. I'd lost but came out not as bad as some would have done. Maybe the shock of me going crazy ape bonkers for self preservation, and the fact that it drew attention from other traffic, meant I came away bloodied and bruised but not too bad, so gave Ian advice to always keep something at your back, never to leave it exposed, try and keep on your feet, *try* being the key word.

Anyway, after a while I just had to ask, "Please can I try on that coat?"

The look of terror on his face: I don't know if he said yes to keep the peace or to be friendly, but I tried on the coat. I was too big for it but managed to get it on. I must have looked like Uncle Fester with his ill-fitting tight coat, and even without saying anything I could see in his eyes, PLEASE DON'T RIP IT, PLEASE DON'T RIP IT. It was a good coat and I didn't say so, but was fecking jealous, very fecking jealous, and guess what? I DIDN'T BLOODY EVER GET ONE – AAAARGH!

Anyway, I gave him back the coat and we all had a chat. It was good to meet Linda again and her young fresh-faced Mod boyfriend and we became good friends. Later I was introduced to another of their friends, Beaker – not the Skin, Beaker, that played in our band – but Vesper Mod Beaker. They were A1, 24 carat Mods, and for a while we all got close, but like human beings do, we drift apart or lose contact, or people just decide they don't want to be around you any more. It's sad but true. I do see Ian and Linda in *The Turks* (pub) and strange Beaker when we see *The HighWasters*, but other things and other people influence everybody. I'm just glad I met them and know them. CHEERS FOR BEING FRIENDS.

The Christmas Tree

Every Christmas Eve we used to get together and have a massive piss-up. It was the done thing to get pissed, have a laugh, go home and wait for the morning to open prezzies. On this particular night we all met up at a pub called *The World Turned Upside Down* (later to become one of those horrible Hungry Horses) and it was to be a good night. Dan and I got there nice and early, about 7ish. It was going to be filled with the Norms from the area, as well as friends: local Skins, Punks and Mods, plus those who would come over from other parts of Reading for the piss-up. The night went well – lots of us in there and the beer going down at rapid speed – then someone put money in the Jukebox and we started trying to sing the Christmas songs we knew, or didn't know in our case, as so many new words and lines were added; but the atmosphere was great and we steadily got drunk.

As the night wore on, we noticed there were lovely decorations but no tree – shame on them – but that just gets the mind going and when you have a lot of mates together, drunk ideas (silly ones) are spontaneous – as the conversation goes on about no tree.

I think Ian West's wife, Linda, said, just in conversation, "It's a shame they didn't get a tree like those over there," pointing to the massive buildings belonging to a company called Gillettes. Yep, the company that makes all the razors and stuff, and on the front ledges of the buildings stood massive Christmas trees and lights.

Well, that was a mistake. Dan, Ian, Beaker, Keith and I all looked at each other and, without another word to anyone else, but chatting excitedly to each other, we left the pub and headed over the road to the tall buildings with a mission in our heads. This was all very well until we reached our objective. It was about 25 feet to the ledges and the trees were close to 20 feet tall as well. Sod it! We scaled the front of the building, all giggling but really with no plan. We reached our goal. Oops – not only are the trees very big but also covered in lights. Electrics!! And no way of turning them off. Add to the fact that none of us had thought about the security hut that was 100 feet down the road, with four guards in it. Oh well, we were pissed and full of Christmas joy, so nothing except electrocution was gonna stop us and, of course, the Bill, if they showed up.

We all looked at each other wondering how to disconnect the lights. Dan and I took the chance. FLICK-CLICK, our gravity knives came out, and without hesitation we cut the wire. No bang – we were both still standing. How? Probably because the handles of these knives were made of real thick oak, and this helped to secure us from the dreaded death by electrocution. Anyway, wires all cut, we got hold of the tree. No, we didn't. It was attached with big staples to the wall. No probs, we dug them out, the tree was free and two Skinheads and four Mods, like a bunch of lumberjacks, pushed the tree to the floor. "TIMBER..." Crash! And still the four security guards had not moved. Why should they? It was Christmas and there was a bunch of drunken Skins and Mods up the side of the building nicking a tree. Who wanted to get hurt? I think a blind eye must have been turned, as we must have been heard the other end of town, giggling and bashing about.

We climbed down and all took hold of the tree, which was bigger than we thought; it must have been close to twenty feet tall. We then ran holding the tree across the road and towards the pub. The oncoming traffic must have had a near heart attack seeing a bunch of nutters running across a road with a giant Christmas tree. By this time others from the pub had seen what we'd done and they were pissing themselves with laughter and egging us on. So we got across the road with the tree, still laughing our heads off. What next? Straight through the pub doors, and the tree just kept going on and on, the top of it ended up at the bar, the end was still outside. All our mates and friends were over the moon, ecstatic with joy. The people who didn't know us looked disgusted but they weren't about to say anything, not with Skins, Mods and Punks pissed up and having fun, but as we were all standing outside admiring our work, the inevitable happened, and the Bill arrived in force.

Cars, vans all over the place. They did their norm; just arrived and ran around with no plan, grabbing hold of anyone about. But they had a shock; we weren't running away. We weren't bothered; we were around the tree singing Crimbo songs. Remember, back then there were no mobile phones. We knew the pub didn't phone the plod, so we hadn't any clue who did. Maybe it was the security guards, but we would never find out and at that time of night and drunk we didn't care. So there we were, all stood about, the plod were scratching their heads and asking the landlady what had occurred. But, Hey Ho, the Christmas gods were on our side; she said she didn't have a clue who'd done it or where they'd gone.

Got to admit the landlady at the time had a bit of a crush on me; she was nice, but I think I only had about three conversations with her. She left not long after this happened (probably because of what happened that night) but all we had to do was help take the tree from the pub and place it on the grass outside; it was up to whoever to collect it.

Dan, Me, Beaker, Ian and Keith all went our merry ways to open prezzies later on, and I'm always going to blame Linda for it, because if it wasn't for her coming out with her innocent observation it would never have happened...YEAH, RIGHT.

Another Christmas Piss-up

As I've said, once upon a time a few of us were real close, and every year we got together for the Christmas piss up, and this particular year was no different to the previous ones; we were going to have fun. Dan, and his girlfriend Lisa (Mod), Ian and his wife, Linda (both Mods), Beaker (Mod), me and my wife (Denise), Keith and, I think his then girlfriend, Sam, were all going to meet up in a pub called the Carousel.

This was the pub of choice for the night, four Mods, two Skins, a Herbert-cum-Boot boy and two very normal girls, not into any cult, one being a diamond: my wife. Dan, me and wifey got there early, as usual, at 7pm on the dot and we made for the long settee that ran along the back wall. We got our drinks and waited for the others to turn up, which was around about 7:30 when they did come in, got their drinks and joined us. Then we started our usual drinking binge for Christmas.

As we got drunker, we got louder; this in turn brought more people from the area, who knew us, to come over and join in the fun, singing and mucking about – the works. It was going great. As we got drunker, as was the norm for Crimbo Eve, someone I didn't know pulled out a can of silly spray string. Well, it was Crimbo, you do silly things – squirt squirt, not maliciously, just covering a few of us. We laughed, but more cans came out and before long about eight of us had cans, then it started; we went completely crazy ape bonkers, everything and everyone around us got sprayed. There was loads of the stuff and we didn't care. We were all drunk, nobody got angry (so we thought) and we had spent loads of money.

Back then, the pubs closed at 11 o'clock, and everyone had to be out by 11:30, so when it was close to that time we all started to leave. We had sprayed so much silly string it hung from all of us. Still, there didn't seem anything wrong. As we were leaving, I saw the settee we were all sitting at covered from one end to the other, and all the tables that we had gathered around us, even the glasses were full, and already the landlord and lady were being called over by some do-gooders in the pub to look, but we were on our merry way: Crimbo pressies to open and all that goes with it.

Anyway, Boxing Day came round and Dan and I decided to go for a crafty afternoon pint, in the Carousel. We went up to the bar and before we could order a pint, we heard, "Your lot is barred."

Dan and I just looked at each other, puzzled, then asked why. A finger pointed to where we were sitting, "Go and look at the damage all that string caused." So we did go and look. Oops – some of the stuff had reacted to the settee and stained the seats, not a great deal but some stains, probably because it was so old and mucky anyway.

"Okay, sorry and all that, but it wasn't deliberate," I said.

"Don't care, you're barred."

Well, Dan and I just looked at each other again and both had the same thought; we had not been rude, or acted like troublemakers in that pub and we got barred for having Crimbo fun. Fuck it! If we are to be barred, let's do it properly. We both grabbed as many glasses as we could and threw them at the mirrors behind the bar and at the shite who had barred us. Nobody tried to stop us, everyone in there just ducked.

"Now you can bar us," Dan said, and we walked out. We just couldn't believe what happened, there had been people in the pub that night who had puked everywhere, smashed glasses, and even someone pulled the water pipes off the wall in the gents (deliberate or not, it was done). All we did was spend loads of money and have a silly string war. Fuck it, a shit pub anyway.

The Bee

Every now and then in life you get pinched by the Old Bill for something stupid, most Skins and Punks I know have been, and this is about my time.

I like bees, the buzzy kind – love them, and I don't know why they like me, must be because I realise that the symbiotic relationship we have with them is needed for survival, but I hate wasps, the flying stripy, stinging kind, not the Rugby team. Why? Well, when Dan and I were about ten and eleven, we were in a park and we saw some big boys by a tree, lighting a fire. We went over and watched. Oh what a silly mistake; it was a wasp nest inside and from the top of the tree came hundreds of wasps. The big boys thought they were dealing with bees and had seen programmes about fire and smoke which calmed bees, as they wanted honey. Well, there weren't any bees, just nasty, horrible wasps who now wanted anybody or anything to sting. They swarmed and attacked – mayhem – everybody legged it. You guessed it, me and Dan were swarmed, taking off running at warp speed, but we were caught, stung to pieces, and Dan was hospitalised because of the attack. We hate wasps!

Anyway, I digress. Dan and I had gone downtown midweek to have an afternoon's entertainment in the local watering hole we used, The Osborne Arms. Not a lot of folks about; I think we only met up with Nikki Parr (A1 Wren) and another whom I can't remember but, anyway, we hit the boozer and got drunkish – not over the top but very very tipsy. Afterwards, we headed for the station where Nikki and the other girl left to go home. Dan and I headed for the little kiosk that sold tea, coffee and bacon rolls all day; we then decided to walk home, Shanks's pony today. As we got to the IDR, the lights were red and, for a change, instead of dodging the cars and running across the road, we waited. Must have been a special day, hardly any traffic; then I noticed a bloody great big bumble bee getting lower and slower to the ground, then thud, or whatever noise a bee makes when it crashes. It was just there in the road about twenty feet from us two. Well, it must have been the beer or the fact that I'm just stupid. I strolled out into the road, got down on my knees and started shoving the bee with a finger to get it to walk onto my other hand. I was not letting it get killed. By now the traffic had started to appear again, but this time they had two pissed-up skinheads in the middle of the road, and one was on his knees. Dan was directing the traffic around – well, giving back the abuse we were both getting. It didn't take long before the Plod appeared, a van load again; they came over. "What you two doing?" one asked.

"Saving a bee," I replied.

"Yeah, saving a bee," Dan said, as about four Plod came over and we got things like, "don't talk shit to us." "What you up to?" Then, as they got nearer, they saw that I'd managed to get the bee into my hands and a big smile was on my face, but as I got over my triumph I saw a couple of Plod go to my bro and two came for me, "Well you're being nicked, for obstruction."

"Well, that's going to look good in court, saving a fucking bee and getting nicked," Dan said.

"It's obstruction, also jaywalking, and which one of you did that?" One of the plod pointed to the road where SKINS AND PUNKS, had been sprayed on the road.

"You having a laugh, mate?" I asked, "It's been there for about a month and can you see any paint spray with us?"

Well, the logic was too much for the coppers and they decided, even though we were drunk, we still had a tad more common sense than they did (except for being in the road), but still they nicked us. Well, Dan and I could have gone mental and run for a bit, but one of us would have fallen over; we were drunk. But before we were cuffed and dragged to the van I did manage to put the bee in the bush on the roundabout, then both of us were put into the van and the short distance to the station, booked in, statements taken and cells awaited, we were put into adjoining cells, so regardless of their threats we had a chat. We both agreed mum and dad and my missus were going to go mental again regardless of the bee-saving, and we both were upset because our boots had been removed and left outside the cell. Having cold feet in a smelly cell is not nice. We were in there for about an hour or so, when we were both taken out and brought into a room where the on duty top notched officer was. We were seated and he then gave us a lecture on stupidity and cheek to the police. We just sat and listened, nodded our heads, accepted his speech; we just wanted to go home. Just charge us and be done, we both thought, but to our surprise he said we were getting a warning and were being released. Well, fuck me, they could have just done that without the headmaster speech, but I suppose they had to have some moral victory. They knew we didn't spray paint the road (never did find out who, we didn't even know) and to go to court for saving a bee, even back then when Skins were public enemy number one, would have looked stupid, but we were both released and a walk home sobered us up. My missus and mum and dad never knew... until now.

Doing Stuff

Sometimes you do things and get away with them; sometimes you do similar things and get nicked, and other times you get asked by someone to do something, knowing you're gonna get nicked but – hey it's worth it.

1994: I'd gone round Dan's place just to have a chat and a drink; nothing important, just two brothers having a chit-chat and beer.

About 5 o'clock in the afternoon there was a knock at the door. When Dan opened it there was this young lady standing there with a little girl by her side. The lady was a Munchkin, probably not even five foot tall. I heard this voice from Dan's open door:

"Excuse me, but are you Danny?" this voice said.

"That depends who's asking and who you are." Dan said.

On hearing this I made for the door, and that's when I saw this Hobbit type young lady with this little girl by her side. She looked at me surprised, but then said,

"Sorry to knock on your door – you don't know me. I live round the road by Debbie (a lady we both knew). I've only been there two weeks, but I'm having trouble and she said to come and see you."

Dan looked at me and I shrugged my shoulders. He invited her and the little girl in and told her I was his brother, and as she sat down he asked her to explain. She said she had moved in round the road to be near Debbie with whom she had made friends. There was just her and her young daughter. She told us her name was Anne-Marie.

We ended up calling her Toto like the little dog from the film, *The Wizard of Oz*, because she was so small like the Munchkins, but we didn't know any Munchkin name and we'd forgotten the name of the major character, *Dorothy*, so Toto we named her. They had moved into a house next door to some known addicts: a whole family of them, a mother and two sons and all the scum that came round to use drugs in that house.

Dan knew them, as he'd had some trouble with them a few months before. They continued to play loud music late into the night and the other neighbours around them were scared. One night when he came home from the pub, Dan had heard the noise and went round to explain to them that if they kept on he would shut them up. He had warned them that next time he came round they would suffer. That night the music had gone off, but they didn't think he or anybody would really act.

She explained that she had asked them to keep the noise down at night, as it was keeping the little one up, and also to stop letting the people they had round the house jump in and out of her back garden and keep banging her windows late at night. She was scared and didn't know who to ask for help. The police, as usual, could not get them out. It had to go through the courts and that would take ages whilst the neighbours would suffer even more.

Dan and I listened, but didn't say we would do anything that night. She broke our hearts, if being honest – she really was scared. But as she left, Dan told her that if we saw them we would ask them to take it down a notch and be more respectful.

When she had left Dan looked at me and said, "If they start tonight, Spike, I'll fucking kill 'em."

I'd had beer and was ready for a bit of aggro, but I really hoped they would behave themselves that night. I just had a bad feeling.

It got to about 10 30pm and I was thinking of going home. We were sitting out in Dan's back garden when a horrible noise started disturbing the atmosphere. It was coming from the other side of the street. This house was twelve houses away. It was them. Dan just grinned.

"C'mon, Spike, those fuckers need sorting."

Well what could I do? My brother had gone into operation kill mode, and I had to stay with him no matter what. No matter how I now felt about violence and trouble, he was my brother and a fellow Skin. TO HELL AND BACK.

We went up to his bedroom and Dan opened the lock-up. All the toys were still in there. We each got a CS gas spray and a rounders bat (this bat is a miniature version of a baseball bat and could easily fit down your trousers or the inside of a jacket, about the size of a police truncheon). We also had a couple of balaclavas – why I don't know – we were going to storm some house in Docs, braces and Brutus shirts – it wouldn't be hard to guess who we were. We also had some old service gloves, the ones you wore in Belfast: black leather with a padded top that covered the knuckles. It was useful to fit some bits of lead strips in this; you could then give a serious backhander.

"So what's the plan then, something tactful or just steam the Bastille?" I said.

"Fuck a plan, Spike, I'm just going to knock on the front door and go mental."

I just laughed , but that was the fact: it was to be special.

We walked round to the house. It wasn't hard to just follow the shitty, inaudible music coming from the place; God knows how anyone could stand it. As we got near, we saw some lads going into the house; they were wobbling all over the place, totally off their heads and swearing. All the windows were open and the noise was deafening.

We both went straight up to the front door, and we put the balaclavas on. Dan pulled his gas out and held it in one hand and a bat in the other. I did the same.

"You ready?" he said.

I nodded. The beer we had been drinking all afternoon had nullified all reasonable action and left us with the alcohol-fuelled need for violence. BANG, BANG, BANG! Dan kicked the door. No response. BANG! BANG! BANG again! This time the door started to open. That was the green flag to go.

Dan pushed the door open as quickly as he could. He sprayed whoever it was at the door with the gas and, as the person went backwards, holding their face, coughing, spluttering and screaming with the stuff taking effect – WALLOP – he hit them with the bat. As I moved into the empty spot now made by the damaged druggy on the floor, I noticed it was a woman of about 40ish: the mother, but she wasn't going anywhere.

I moved straightaway into the kitchen that was in front of me. As I went through the door, there was a teenager there of about 17 or 18. He was off his trolley, standing by the fridge. I just sprayed him with gas and hit him with the bat. He went straight to the ground where I kicked him a couple of times. I left the kitchen and went to where my brother had gone: the living room. The noise had stopped as Dan had smashed the stereo with the bat and thrown the speakers out of the window. All this had taken less than a minute.

We then both turned to go up the stairs. As we started up, three lads were coming down. The music had stopped and they were coming to see why. It was the two brothers and a drugged-up friend. They just looked shocked. We just ran up the stairs and, as we got closer, before they could turn and run, we gassed them. Instantly spluttering and coughing. We just laid into them with the bats, smashing them as fast as we could. They crumpled on the stairs, screaming for us to stop. We then kicked them down the stairs and, as we followed them, the mother was getting back on her feet. WHACK! I just kicked her straight in the side, and she went back down. Two of the three we'd just attacked were out cold; the third, Dan was dragging out of the front door. I followed and as I got outside Dan had him round the throat.

"Listen, you drugged-up fuck. I've warned you – you didn't listen. Now I'm gonna tell you this once. You and your drugged-up mother and brother bring any more scum round here and make this shitty noise and disturb the neighbours, and I'll come back and cut all your throats – believe me I will!"

The dickhead just looked up, bleeding from his head and mouth and said,

"YOU'RE FUCKING DEAD. WAIT TILL I TELL MY MATES – I KNOW WHO YOU TWO ARE. YOU'RE DEAD!"

What a mistake to make. We were already in bloodlust mode, and now he had threatened me and Dan. WALLOP! WALLOP! Two more whacks with the bat – this time across the shoulders. He started to cry.

"Okay, okay, STOP – we won't, we won't – sorry!" he said.

Personally, I don't even think he could spell sorry, let alone know what it meant. Then as I looked up and around me, I saw the local neighbours had come out and were standing by the front garden fence all watching – old and young people. Well we're fucked now, I thought; half the fucking street have seen what's going on and, being the only two skinheads in the area, it wasn't hard to pick me and Dan out. As we both turned around to go, one of the neighbours – an old guy about 60ish, stopped us. He had tears in his eyes.

"THANKS, LADS, WE COULDN'T HAVE DONE ANYTHING."

Dan and I had to get away fast, although this lot watching appreciated what we had done, there is always one person who just has to grass you up and phone the plod, and the sirens were already screaming our way.

We walked a little up the road and dumped the gas sprays into a dustbin in a garden. The bats we were about to throw, when Toto came out.

"Give me those," she said. "I'll give them back later." She took the bats and balaclavas. Sorted: no weapons to take back. All we had to do was sit tight back at Dan's house and wait for Plod.

Dan and I both knew, if arrested, we were probably going to get done heavily by the plod and possibly prison time. Well, I phoned the missus just to say I was still at Dan's and might stop the night. Couldn't leave him on his own now, and if the plod knew it was him, they wouldn't just knock the door for us to answer, they would do as usual, steam the place, cause as much damage as they could, give us a kicking and nick us both.

The police had arrived, about two hours had passed and still no plod at the door. Dan and I couldn't work it out. What are they up to, we thought? Then, about one in the morning we heard a tap at the door. That really shit us up, a little tap tap. We both looked out the windows, couldn't see the plod but it could be them lying in wait. I went with Dan to the door and he opened it. There was Toto.

"You're in the clear. We told the police it was some lads in a van that jumped out and steamed the house."

We just both laughed. "They believed you lot, and not the shits in the house?" I said.

"The one Danny threatened couldn't be sure it was him and you. He was so out of his head, he didn't know for sure. He kept on saying it was him from around the road."

Well, lucky for us that evening the two drugged-up shits and their mates had had an argument with a family around the road and they had threatened them, but how he got them mixed up with me and Dan I'll never know. They were smellies (rockers) and we had just attacked, albeit with Balaclavas on, in boots, braces and Brutus shirts. But, hey, who was complaining if those twats were so out of their brains they couldn't tell who from what. Fuck 'em. And the Bill, for a change, were not too concerned; they knew the trouble this lot were and, I think, they were pleased to see them all hurt.

But the law is the law, and even fucking druggies are supposed to be protected. Needless to say, there wasn't any noise from their place again. In fact, in less than a month, they were out of the house. Where they went, fuck knows. Who cares? A hole would have been too good for them. But the funny thing was, about a week before they went, the

170

mother came round one evening. Dan and I were just going out when she turned up. She actually asked Dan and me to give her sons a good hiding, as they had hit her. What a family! We didn't do it; we told her we didn't want anything to do with that kind of violence. About a year ago, I found out the mother had died of an overdose and one of the brothers had HIV. Well, there you go. These people play with fire and sometimes they get burned. In my view not often enough.

2004 Fiji Toffs

Mumsy wanted me to go to her house, then out for a beer with her, Tom (stepdad, Welsh, good lad) and Dan, to the local village drinking hole for my birthday. Sounded okay (this is when I still drank; stopped in 2009) but ever since I hit my 40s I'd given up with birthday bashes. I made arrangements to go for the weekend and stay with Mumsy and Dan; the missus never came any more to my drinking missions. I think over the years she got fed up watching many Skins and friends getting drunk and probably having a tad fisticuffs with some prats that had too much and fancied taking the piss out of old Skins like Dan and me, and whoever we were with, plus Missus had not drank for many years. She stopped in about '89 and hadn't touched a drop. It takes willpower, as I have found out since I stopped.

Got to Mum's. Dan was polishing his boots and Mum and Tom were pottering about. Dan and I were going to go down the pub for mid afternoon and then the marathon would take place. Well I'd try. The little place we were going to was a traditional village pub. It had its regulars and what they thought were their naughty local boys, the odd fisticuffs or vandalism. Dan was totally in a different league and they knew it. Every time we both turned up there, it was like Ron and Reggie Kray to them. We had so many stories and, after a few beers, the locals loved to sit down and listen. Oh, how the big world really works.

Mum had told me, as always, to keep a lookout for Dan. He had been diagnosed with Huntingdons by this time and he had changed. Anything could set him off, and with his meds it was like playing Russian roulette at times, and he could not drink like he used to, but as big brothers do, I'd keep an eye out, because the fabulous Doctors from the Churchill hospital in Oxford could no longer keep him out of prison if he got into trouble, and he would go down for a long time. Even the small-minded Bill for the local village had it in for us. They knew, unlike the locals, that we wouldn't take any shite from them. Yeah, if we did get out of order and were nicked, so be it, but not without a fucking fight.

What a result. There was a rugby tournament on telly all day, and the pub was full of the local team, (songs and beer to be had) and from just up the road a load of New Zealanders and Aussies. They all came over to work in a sawmill type place. Year in-year out they would come: mostly good lads, good workers and boy could they fucking drink. I don't know why the Maori's that came over really liked Dan and me; they said we weren't a picture or false, that what you saw is what you got. Cheers, lads.

The day was going good. Many beers had been drunk and the laughs were beginning as the alcohol took its effect: watching the rugby, taking the piss out of each other, the Aussies taking it from the English and the Kiwi's, the Scots and Welsh from everyone, and the Paddies the brunt of anything funny. Great afternoon; just what I needed and, for Dan, loads of beer, rugby, and no animosity at all. Then it happened.

Two lads had walked in. They went over to the Aussies and Kiwi's; they just seemed different.

I asked Dan, "Do you know them two who just walked in?"

"Yep, they are with that lot from the mill, but they are from Fiji, rich boys, but they think they are like them."

"But they are white lads," I said.

"Mummy and Daddy are loaded, sent them round the world for a year, but they have stayed here. The Kiwi's say they are lazy shits, don't like hard work; you know the sort, Spike."

Well, that says it all really. Why do hard work when you're minted;

just go round the world making out you're working and try and blend in with the oinks for a year or two.

An hour or two went by. Party atmosphere, good laughs, and I went to the bar for my umpteenth real ale. As I was standing there, one of the Fiji lads (the younger of the two) was at the bar. He was already looking smashed. I ordered my beer and turned to see the rugby on telly.

"I hope the French beat the English," came out of his mouth.

I looked at him, took a moment to take in what he just said (beer, it slows the mind).

"You what mate, why? Nothing against the French, but this is an English pub and full of mostly English."

"Yeah, but it's good to see them get beat. Arrogant some of those Brits," he said.

I just looked at him again. Did he really mean that? Do I lose it or try and see if he is just on a wind-up. I turned round, paid for the ale and looked at him again.

"Who's arrogant? Those rugby players or all Brits? You serious?" I asked.

"Well, mostly the English. No offence mate, but the English are arrogant," he said, slurring.

"SO WHY ARE YOU HERE THEN? WHAT YOU DOING IN ENGLAND?"

By now my heckles were up and I was staring at him. He just had a stupid look on his face, and I could tell he was two parts pissed. I still couldn't work out if he was too pissed to realise what he was saying, really stupid, or out for confrontation.

With a stupid grin he said, "My brother and me are over here for a year's work, with all those up there at the mill, but I don't really like it. It's just for a year though, then I'll get out of this shit hole."

"Well, you're lucky, mate. Some of us don't have a rich Mummy and Daddy. Yeah, I know you're loaded, and I have to work hard for a

174

living."

As I finished the sentence I turned to put the ale on the bar. I knew the next shit that came out of his mouth would then be followed by a right uppercut.

As I was just turning my head towards him, I saw Mum and Tom coming into the bar and, as I continued to turn towards this prat, he just came at me, glass in hand. Luck, quick movement, or he was just too stupid and drunk to do what he had planned. His glass just bumped the side of my head, but I had him. SMASH! I head-butted him in the nose — whoosh — blood everywhere, and I grabbed him by the shoulders and threw him and myself to the floor, landing on top of him and heard the air just gush out of his lungs. He was in pain and I knew it, and now I was gonna hurt him.

As this was happening, my Mum had just screamed. The pub had gone quiet for a moment before all ran towards the rumpus, including my brother. Oops, his head had gone.

By this time I'd grabbed one of the Fiji's arms and had twisted it until it snapped and, as he tried to wiggle away, I bent it back and squeezed with all my strength and his shoulder then snapped too (as I was to be later informed). I was then gonna stand up and just go boot-dancing on him, but I was grabbed and pulled to the bar. "Stop, stop, no, no, no more please," was coming from mouths and faces. I don't know who grabbed me. I was so mad.

Mum was swearing by now and, as in her manner, heading for the twat crying in pain on the floor. Tom held Mum, thank God, but then as they all concentrated on me, and my Mum trying to calm us down — SMASH! They had taken no notice of Dan. He had a stool in his hands and crashed straight into the twat's brother, who was trying to get his brother to a back door. He didn't stop — another stool and SMASH he tried to hit them both. Luckily for them, he hit the wall. It exploded with the force and covered them in bits of stool.

Everybody then turned and ran for Dan, but by now he had grabbed two giant ash trays and with one in both hands attacked. They grabbed him just in time, but he was still trying to put the boot in as they dragged him away. Mayhem was everywhere: screams, shouts, crying, but there you go; if it wasn't for this twat nothing would have happened and it would have been a good night.

Mum and Tom by now were with Dan and calming him down. He just had a wicked grin on his face, so I found out later. The lad I hit, his brother had said as he was picking him up, that he'll sort that bloke out, don't worry. Well, Dan had heard this and while on his mission to attack the twat I hit, he went into massacre mode and attacked both. Well you have to; in those situations it's look after No. 1 and family and friends. It's the adrenalin and from being in those situations before. These two were just rich boys who thought money and the attitude we've got digs them out of the shit. Maybe it does to weak bods, and usually I don't give a fuck about people slagging down the English. We probably have deserved it from our past, but I *am* English and I love this country − not its politics − this country and what it means. Some rich twat from some part of the world who has been spoilt for all his life is not gonna take the piss out of me, family, or the country. NO.

Well, needless to say the aftermath was expected. They went to the plod who then steamed the pub about an hour and a half after the rumpus. They just wanted an excuse to nab Dan and me. It was funny; they came in numbers in riot gear. YEAH, RIOT GEAR just to nick us. Dan and me just laughed − about twelve cops in gear just to take us on. I think it was an excuse just to wear their armour. Well all they usually nicked were pissed-up farmers and shoplifters, so a good night for them. We went peacefully, although my Mum wanted to take on the armoured assault that came into the pub.

The first thing on my mind was: *Oh no, what do I say to the Missus? I'm in trouble*. Well yep, I got in trouble with her, but she calmed down a tad when told it was the two others that started it, but end result was a five year suspended sentence. Luckily, all the Maori's had come to my defence and told the court it was a case of self-defence. He attacked me, and I took all the blame, even for Dan's attack. He would have gone down; that was a cert, and the two rich boys — well the Aussies and Kiwi told them to fuck off. They didn't want anything to do with them.

As one of the Kiwi's said, "You don't get the rozzers involved when you have started a ruck. It's wrong. You either sort it or shut up."

Well, you cannot say more than that and I suppose these two, if not back on their island by the beach, telling stories about being attacked by English Skins, they are doing something very worthy like FUCK ALL, – just wishing they could be real men, and anyway I could have got a lot worse. I made up my mind after that I'm too old and can't afford trouble any more.

Teds RockaBillies and PsychoBillies

Anyone of my age would probably have had parents being Teds or even the original Mods. My Mum and Dad were 1950s Teds and I grew up with the music and all the stories about the goings on that went with it. I didn't know any others, and the first contact I ever had with them was with my Aunty who used to take me to the Punk gigs, (when I was still a Punk 76-77). She knew loads, so when I bumped into them on the way to gigs I got off lightly with only some leg pulling, all because of my Aunty, but I must say that I did admire them; they did take pride in what they were wearing, clothes as well as that greased-up hair do. No matter how it looked, you have to admit they took pride.

Then one evening after a gig, I was on the way home. My Aunty had gotten off the bus one stop before me. I was still with a few others so everything was okay. But, oh dear, as we got to our stop and got off there were a load of Teds: blokes and women. There had been a 50's music night at a local hall and loads had come. It was like *Custer's Last Stand*. As we got off the bus, they just abused us and then – crunch! – we took a kicking. "Get the Punks" was all I heard and I had never run so fast to get away and home: a mess, a bloody nose and face and my arse was killing me as I was kicked by one of those Ted girls with stiletto shoes. But later, when I had turned Skin, I and other mates got our revenge in Southend on the bank holidays of 78-79. If you were there, you know what I mean. But I have no animosity towards them; I like them; they have style. But that's what sub culture cults do – a dust-up every now and then, arguments and confrontations, and at the time let's face it as skinheads we fought them all. But as I've said before, have had many conversations with Teds, and the ones who lost it when I mentioned *Showaddywaddy* really put what they thought over; they hated them. I haven't seen many for years now. No doubt there are clubs and crews of them around who just don't die. They are a massive part of subculture history of this country and the world.

Rockabilly

The first one I ever met was a lad called Billy. Fancy, a rockaBilly called Billy. He was a good bloke. It was probably 1979 and he could handle himself, and if he ever was in a pub where we were and there was trouble, he would use his fighting skills with us lot. As I saw them, they were the skinheads of the Teds, harder looking, rougher. Yep, Teds might argue, but that's how I and we saw them. Their music was also more down-to-earth. That double bass sound and drum stood out from the normal rock 'n roll of the Teds.

I didn't have a lot of contact with this side of Rock 'n rollers, and I must say every time I saw some or bumped into any I knew, we had a good conversation. Personally, all the time I've been Skin (fingers crossed) have never had any trouble with RockaBillies. I even like RockaBilly music, and so many Skins, if they grew their hair for court, or just didn't want to be Skin any more, would have a flat top, just like all the RockaBillies. It does look smart, even when the hair has been bleached, which was a craze during the 80s. Got to admit I've come across more RockaBillies during my 40s and now in my 50s than I did when I was young. I'm not saying there are more now; it just seems luck I suppose that I bump into them. Long may I do so; again, a sub culture that bloomed here in England and a lifestyle born.

Psychobillies

Now this lot I couldn't get my head around: a mixture of Punk and RockaBilly? Where did that come from? Considering the hate during the 70s and early 80s of the Teds and RockaBillies trying to bash the shit out of Punks, it was crazy. It must have been round about 1980 when I first came across them. We were all going to some Ska party in Bristol and met them as we came out of the station. At first I thought they were Punks, and I don't know why it suddenly went off. For about five minutes we bashed the shit out of each other, and five minutes continuous fighting is a long time. The Bill or something usually stops it after a minute or so. That was the first introduction to PsychoBilly, and we had many more confrontations with them. I never ever asked what the Teds or RockaBillies thought about them; I could imagine the Teds being outraged, wearing all that Punk style gear with 50s haircuts and colours and having the name Billy in their sub culture name. But I must say that, like Punk, they stood out, and again, a subculture made in England that has bloomed and survived. I do still see PsychoBillies about and they bring a smile to my face; it seems they are still strong in numbers, but I couldn't tell you any band they like now. The only one that I knew was *King Kurt*, and that band always made me smile. Load of nutters and everybody knew the song, *Destination Zulu Land*.

Bootboys and Herberts

These names have stayed with me since I was a lad. I don't know if they were just words used in London, down south, south-east, central south-west and the West Country, but as I grew up they referred to Jack-the-Lad blokes: the tough nuts. So when I got to teenage and beyond, into Punk then Skin, these names were used a lot. For us it meant the lads who were not Skins or Punks, but hung around with us, always in boots, and any jacket: Ma1s, Harringtons, Crombies, or leather jackets with their turned-up jeans. They would stand by us in fights and come along to gigs. I suppose these were an underclass subculture, something yet to metamorphose into its own thing.

The word, Bootboys, was also used for Skins, but there were lads who were genuine Bootboys. I can see them now with their DMs and turned-up jeans; longish hair, some of them, others a little spiky, and some had the popular mullet of the 70s and this long, leather, duster type coat. I can remember, as a young kid, in the the early 70s at football, seeing these, and also during the football violence of the late 70s. If it wasn't Skins it was the Bootboys.

I haven't seen Herberts or Bootboys for years; maybe because the Skin and Punk thing has gone underground now, and is not so popular as in the late 70s and 80s. So these two subcults have either died or become hidden from view. I hope when the gangster craze has finally died a death on the streets of this country, the youth will get back to wearing proper street clothing again and, on the street corners, will be the Bootboy or Herbert. At least his trousers will be around his waist and not showing his arse or wearing a stupid hoodie.

Smoovies

An unprovoked attack

These were the normals, the ones that went to all the night clubs, dressed in the fashion of the disco boys of the day, listened to the popular Radio 1 crap or what the media told them was the in thing. Of all the cults – if you call them a street cult – these gave me (us) the most aggravation. I couldn't really get my head around them; some of them used to be Skins, Punks, Bootboys or Herberts. They would go to football on a Saturday and cause violence; they would be spouting ring wing chants at the football, but then at night time be friendly to any ethnic race that made them look like their friends – probably just to get the drugs they were now into. They would even be around the Irish smoovies who were dragged into the IRA support because their dad or mum, or even the pet dog they had was from Ireland, or because they had an Irish name, but they had to be anti Brit or English, and then the smoovies would all come together to have a go at us. We had loads of punch-ups with this lot and, as I've said one time, I think we could have been killed in Southend when we were caught in the open by hundreds of the twats.

What I don't understand is: the lads and girls that did eventually give up Skin or whatever, changed straightaway into one of the enemies we had trouble with – talk about double standards. I can remember one night; Dan and I and two other Skins (sorry lads I can't remember your names now) were taking Dan's girlfriend and her mate back to the train station. It was late, pubs closed, the only place open being the night club around by the station. But we got the girls (Punks they were)

184

safely on to the train with no probs. As we came out, we headed for home, no buses, long walk (those bloody days in the late 70s and 80s when everything stopped after 11 o'clock: pubs, buses, et al).

As we walked past the night club, there were a load of smoovies coming out: black and white, and with them were two blokes who used to be skinheads. Dan and I saw them; we even waved a hand to them in acknowledgement. The next thing, they pointed to us and a load of smoovies just attacked, led by a group of blacks. There was nowhere to go. One of the Skins with us just took off like a cheetah – whoosh – gone; his bottle just went. The three of us that were left had to fight for our lives and, just to add to our bad luck, as they came towards us they went past a building site and, bugger me, they all picked up bits of four by two – bad to worse.

Well, we stood our ground but took a beating, and I will say some of them got stabbed, by whom I'll never say, but in that situation, you'll do anything to protect yourself and those with you. Dan and I did get a beating with the wood. Dan was knocked unconscious when he was hit in the head; I just covered him with my body and took the beating. Thankfully, I think some of those that were stabbed ran, and the others then followed; the Bill were on their way and *they* didn't get nicked we usually did.

Anyway, I got Dan to his feet with the help of the other lad who battled that night, and we knew we had to get to the hospital. We walked all the way to A&E and, as we limped through the door, we just got pushed straight to the front and dragged in. We were just covered in blood. Dan's head was split open. He ended up with sixteen stitches in the head; he also had the bones of one of his hands sticking through his skin as well as a broken arm, and other cuts and bruises. I had a broken arm and hand. We both had lost teeth. As well as other cuts and bruises, I also had a wound in my lower back where I had been stabbed and didn't know it; it had just missed my spine. The other lad was a tad luckier; only a kicking he took, but we would all be black and blue for some time.

Needless to say we got our revenge later when we got back to norm, and those two that turned on us old skinheads. Turning on old mates; they were never to be forgotten. Everyone got to know who they were, never to be trusted again, and anyway, one went from a back-stabbing, two-faced shit, to being a rapist. He will one day get what he deserves – a painful death.

Skinhead for me has changed a lot. It was and is destroying itself; all because of politics, there is a massive divide to extreme right and left, and Skins are knocking the shit out of each other, just because of a flag and rich wankers directing and controlling Skins like puppets. It's got to stop – we have to take our cult back! Two fingers up to the wankers using us as their strong arm; it's about mates, music, good times and an odd punch-up because we are Skins, not politically controlled robots.

Why do I say this? It's because, as a young Skin, I was dragged into politics. I thought those all around me were genuine, would look after me as they said if I got into trouble with the law, and earn money with the band, extreme right wing like many I got into. I will say some of the things we got up to were a fucking laugh, the gigs were a buzz never to be forgotten and I don't regret those, but I soon found out the lies behind the faces giving me the orders, or supposed to be making me money.

They let me and my brother down, left us to defend ourselves when we got in trouble for crimes for them. Okay they *were* crimes and we got caught, so be it: you do the crime and do the time, but we were promised all the help, lawyers, et al, and we got nothing not even an excuse as to why. There I learned a massive lesson in life: all politicians are liars, and since that time I've lived by the words, **All Politicians Are Criminals** and **All Politics is Criminal**. On my post box, for any and all political parties is a sign that reads:

"ANY and ALL POLITICIANS of ANY PARTY, PLEASE DO NOT LEAVE ANY of YOUR PAMPHLETS or PARAPHERNALIA in MY LETTER BOX. YOUR POLITICS is CRIMINAL and ALL POLITICIANS ARE CRIMINALS. PLEASE TAKE the PAMPHLETS and YOURSELF AWAY and DO WHAT YOU DO BEST ELSEWHERE: LIE."

As I've said to many people in conversations, I'm not anti Fascist and I'm not anti Commi; I'm not pro either. If I were anti or pro any, that would mean I'm into politics and I'm not; neither am I into non-controlled mass immigration or economic migration. It's wrong, but as always we are told by the bods in charge that we have to have it; it's good for us because they say so, and the people in charge of the country never give us a choice, we just do as they say.

Okay, I say if we have to be a multi-cultural society, start telling that to the migrants; it's they who are taking over some districts and saying "no white is welcome", or "we have our own laws not this country's" and they have parts of towns and estates that won't accept an Englishman, black or white, going there, as it is now theirs. Is that multi cultural? NO. The powers that be turn a blind eye to it, because if they did take notice, they would have to accept that there is a massive problem brewing. I don't care who lives here if they become part of society, not little enclaves of Poles, Russians, Muslims, WHATEVER.

'If you're here, you become part of the society that has been around for eons. Yes, be proud of your ethnic race, but you have chosen to be British (English) so now accept where and what you are.'

If they don't, extremism will soon infest everyday life and the country will explode. This is all due to lack of control from the politicians. I say stop faffing about and do what has to be done before it all goes tits up and, every time I say this, I then get called a RACIST. NO. I'm a realist and am not scared to say what many others really think.

During my time as a Skin I've met many different types: just completely stupid, hardened criminals, violent nutcases and even some cowards, but I must say most were a pleasure to have known, even some of the cowards had a valid excuse. Not all people, no matter what uniform they wear, are into violence, or ready to use it at any time. I learned that this is just normal human behaviour and you cannot change what is not there. The criminals amongst us soon left the Skin scene to concentrate on their nocturnal light-fingered habits, and many were soon spending long sentences in a prison, which became their lives. It's not called growing up – it's called stupidity and not having the sense to see right from wrong. These were also the ones that got into the drug culture; they go together: crime and drugs and, again, if you cannot see the right and wrong of that, you get what you deserve. That *Sword of Damocles* hangs over their heads all the time. The nutters, well they were nutty. When they were done with Skin, they ended up the hard cases around town centres or their local pubs, fighting and getting arrested, then getting older and slower, until one day the good hiding they get will leave them seriously ill or dead.

My best mate for all this time being a Skin has been my brother, Dan. We've had so many adventures and laughs, and we trusted each other with each other's lives and Skin for us *meant* our lives. If it were not for the illness that has taken over his and my sister's life, he would still be 24 carat 100% Skin, and we would still be going to disco's (I'm old; I still call them disco's) together. Unfortunately, those days are history for the Pitt brothers, but I'll never forget them and the secrets we still have. It has been an honour and privilege to have been Dan's brother, and to have known him. He was Skin before me and, regardless of his health, I know he will always be a Skin. There is a saying in Latin: *Nulli Secundas* that means second to none. That's what I think of Dan.

In my old age now, I hope violence doesn't come my way. I'm too old for that now; been there, done it, got the T-shirt. I just want good times, although I get some strange looks from young and old when they see a skinhead and an old one to boot.

Although I don't drink any more: 5 years now, I still have a laugh when I go out. I'm just sober doing it. Boy, does it give you a different perspective on gigs and events when you're sober. Now I know what my Missus used to go on about. God, how she put up with me drunk I'll never know, but I suppose being told I had to stop was the best thing to happen. I do miss the odd Ale, but I couldn't afford it now anyway if I did still drink. Since I lost my job through an accident I have not been able to get back into employment, no matter what my experience is. I am regarded as too old and I'm afraid to say no one will employ me.

When I look back at some of the violence, I do wonder how I did it. I know it is a Skin thing and many of us had to have our weekly punch-up, but as a person I'm not a bully. I've always been respectful and polite to anyone. Manners was a big thing instilled in us as young kids and I think that has been lost to the youth of today. I do have a bad and quick temper, but that came from being run over as a kid, and a head injury. Well that's what I'm sticking to. I don't think it was a case of "let's go out and commit wanton violence"; it just came to us. We were and are the hard edge of street cults, and some people and other sects and cults just wanted to have a go.

We didn't win all; most of them, but even Skins can have a bad day or night, and I took as well as dished out some good hidings, from black and white youths, and from the Plod (police), but *they* can get away with most as their uniforms protect them. Being a paid hooligan must be fun.

The one thing I never really enjoyed, or wanted to do, was football violence. I'm not saying I didn't do it. I did. In the mid to late 70s and early 80s it was an epidemic at our football grounds and I was part of that for a time. I just didn't get on with it. For a time the Skin, Bootboy and Herbert kicked the shit out of each other on a Saturday afternoon, but soon some peeps became really into it, organised, and even gave up Skin to dress smoothy (meaning being normal?), so you couldn't distinguish hooligan from ordinary supporter. They had their own dress code now, from the bright track suits of the late 70s early 80s to the *Aquascutum* and *Stone Island* of today, and some people like my friend, Andy Frain became a well known Chelsea and England football hooligan. How he continued with it I'll never know but, as I've said before, I liked him, still do and I like the man not the propaganda by

190

the police and media. For me though, I, like other Skins, left this to continue on our merry way. Saturday afternoons was for beer and a laugh. Not saying every now and then an afternoon's football wouldn't be attended, but it got dodgy for being arrested, and now it wasn't just fines but a prison sentence. No, not for me; my missus would have killed me. As I'm older now, I would like to think I could pass on some of my hard found and fought for wisdom to young Skins but, like all young people, how many actually listen to anyone older – not a lot. And before you know it you're up to your neck in things you cannot change, or being forced to do and choose. But at least some may listen and realise that skinhead is not about political directions; it's about having a laugh with friends and music, bank holiday coastal invasions and maybe the odd punch-up, parties, girls, (if you're lucky) loads of nooky, drinking with people you trust, mutual respect and, of course, the clobber (clothes) and your boots highly polished. Sorry for all you non skinheads, but that is what real Skin was/is like. It all goes together to make a cult enjoyable, and for some a life. I get the odd comment like "Haven't you grown up?" What is grown up? I say look around you – you all dress the same, you talk the same shite and you all vote the same, and you're grown up? You all have just jumped into the ruling bodies' scenario of how they want the masses to behave: all the same, just robots. Individualism and cults they don't like – people don't like it makes them nervous.

Being a Pirate

When we were still in the RAF, Dan and I, Bounce and Taff decided it was time for a holiday. We asked a couple of civvy mates if they were interested and told them the plan. We would hire a canal boat for ten of us and have a week of up and down the rivers and canals of this lovely nation. We would put the money up front for the holiday (we did earn more than our civvy mates). All they would need was money for food and drink. A fabulous great idea and plan.

In the end, ten of us would go: four Skins (us from the camp), Dan and Bounce's girlfriends. Punks, and two Punk mates and their girlfriends who were also Punks. Four Skins, six Punks. Wey-hey — gonna be a laugh. We all got off to Stoke on Trent to collect the Canal boat.

When we got to the company that we hired from, we had some very funny looks. It was okay when I booked it from the camp; an RAF chappy hiring a boat with three other servicemen didn't seem too bad, but we turned up with six Punks, and we had to show our service IDs to prove it was us on the inventory to take possession of the boat.

We were then taken to our boat. Well this caught us out. I was expecting one of those long skinny canal boats; we got something that looked like a mini Titanic without the funnels. Lush wasn't a good enough word; it was long but not skinny, pure white with loads of massive windows. Fabulous it was; could sleep twelve, so no worries about room, and none of us had a clue how to run it properly.

The last time I'd been on a boat was to cross the Thames to get into the festival, and that ended up with a crunch. I should have thought this idea of a holiday out prior to booking – but there you go – young and foolish, but what a fecking laugh this was going to be. We were gonna follow the four counties ring, 110 miles in length cruising, and nearly 100 locks, but we were not in a hurry; didn't have a clue what to do, or in any rush. We had taken ten days off, but the route should have only taken about six days. Well we would see.

The first day, Dan, Bounce, Taff and I took turns taking control of the boat just to get a bit of confidence, and get round all the controls: a steering wheel for the rudder, a control stick that stayed in the middle for stop, push forward, you went forward and all the way back to stop – not too hard, but it was a boat, and water moves. Oh dear, those currents again, but hey – four Skins and also servicemen – no probs. We didn't go too far the first day, just a few miles and a couple of locks, and that was a shocker, the locks, but we managed and then decided to stop and moor up. That's when we found some hammers and big stakes, oh yeah! Smash them into the bank and tie up the boat, as well as the little anchor to throw over the side – no probs we were all now sailors.

That night was just a party: lots of beer that we had brought on, a massive tape deck to play music and annoy the wildlife for miles around, listen to Punk and Ska and nobody to complain – and the girls (well it had to be) to use the cooker to do all the munchies. It would be a holiday of eggs, bacon and sausages and maybe some beans.

That night we made our plan. The route took us along the canals where there were riverside shops and pubs (for food and drink). We would stop at some of these and restock; it seemed the done thing and we would do the same, and the only things we needed were beer, eggs and bacon, bread and the drink that has kept England going: TEA.

Day 2: it started okay. Tea, breakfast, unmoored and pulled up the anchor. Dan would take the boat up to the first stop we could find and restock. I don't know what little place it was, but we came across a pub at the side of the river: result. We managed to stop okay and like a bunch of Vikings we stormed the pub. It was only to be a mid afternoon lunch, if they did food, and a drink or two. Well the drink went down too well and we got to pub shutting time, 2:30 in the afternoon — all of us very, VERY merry and going back to the boat. I don't know why, but Vikings were being talked about; this thought stayed in our minds and, as we got back to the boat, Taff had an idea.

Before I go on, let me tell you about Taff. He was generally a quiet bloke, never said too much and he always spoke slowly and to the point, never much chit-chat. He was a Cardiff born Welshman, about six foot one, but skinny, and very lean. He was from a big family brought up by just his mum; his dad had died at an early age, and he had been bullied, so his mum had sent him to Karate lessons, and he told us he was a black belt. At that time none of us had seen anything of his boasted abilities and Taff had never been in a ruck with us, so we just accepted his boast. Why not — he was a mate? Anyway, Taff had now had a drink and this always changed him; he would just start giggling, come out of his shell and come up with some awesome ideas — and on this day he said, "LETS GO VIKING UP AND DOWN THE CANAL."

Oh dear, a good idea when you're drunk. We plugged in the tape deck, turned the volume up to bleeding ears, unmoored the boat and whoosh, we were off. Well not so much whoosh. I think the boat didn't do over 3mph but whoosh anyway. All this Viking stuff started off okay — just a laugh, and on the Canals there is usually not too much room, so when you go past another boat it's close. We did go past some boats, some banter from us and the odd comment, not very Viking, but we were cracking open the beer, cans and bottles and we were getting wrecked. Bounce was steering the boat and, as we came round a bend, the canal opened up and met a river. I don't know which one, but there was room now for more boats. By now the girls had taken off some clothing to get more of the hot sun. We were all by now just in boots, jeans and braces, very drunk and soaking up the sun. Even the Punk mates had taken off the leather jackets – well for a Punk that was sunbathing.

Anyway, as we were debating if we should stop and just fester on the banks, we heard the girls and by now a very pissed Taff shouting. We looked to where they were shouting and saw a long canal boat, with some men and women on board. They were moored to the bank and had what looked like some gazebos up. It was a party and, at that moment, we didn't know how many people there were. Taff and the girls were shouting abuse over to the other boat, and they were shouting back. It didn't seem too bad – just loud banter, but then a tomato came across from the other bank and we saw other people coming onto their boat and joining in. Well that was the button pushed: Taff and the girls, two parts pissed, just lobbed their cans and bottles over to the other boat, crash, bang as the projectiles hit. At the same time, Bounce just turned the boat and headed for theirs.

"What the fuck you doing," I said.

"FUCKING VIKING ATTACK!" he said. Well, that was that. We all started lobbing our cans and bottles as we headed towards their boat. Oh fuck, I thought as we got nearer; the boat just seemed to get larger and larger – we were going to ram it. I don't know how, but Bounce turned the wheel, slammed it into reverse and turned the wheel again. How he did it I'll never know. It came to a slow controlled joining to the other vessel. As the two boats joined, all of us just jumped on to the other one, screaming, shouting and looking for a target. The men on board had fled and run towards the gazebos. The only people left on the boat were a few girls and the four girls on our side made a beeline for them. Our charge carried on from our boat over theirs and onto the bank. Then we saw what was in front; they had called for support and there must have been about fifteen blokes looking at us. The die had been cast and we couldn't stop now, but before we could lay into them Taff had charged forward, and yep, he could do Karate. It was like watching Bruce Lee; he was marvellous – whoosh, whack, slam, bang, biff, bodies going everywhere, but he was pissed and I suppose his balance just went. He did some sort of kick and crash and went into the tables. That was our cue to charge, help our Bruce Lee friend. It was a typical mayhem pall mall fight, as many punches and kicks taken as ditched out, and anyway we were pissed – it would only hurt tomorrow. Then we heard the dreaded siren: time to leave. We gathered up each other and headed back to the canal boat to then board ours. Fuck, where was our boat? It seemed we had all forgotten that we had come to a stop to do our Viking raid.

But nobody had tied up the boat and the currents were strong, so the BOAT HAD GONE DOWN RIVER. Well now there was nowhere to hide, the girls had started nicking anything not tied down and were still inside the canal longboat. It didn't take the Bill long to get to us. No matter how this all occurred it would have been our fault, and from nowhere there was a little motor boat full of coppers, which still cracks me up today. It had a little blue light on the roof of the cabin and a siren. Where that came from is anybody's guess – we didn't pass a police station on the river – it's just one of those mysteries. Suffice to say we all got nicked.

We got taken to the local nick and all booked in. They had split us up; all the RAF lads put into a big cell and the civvies were spread out, and – fancy – none of the others had been nicked, even though they'd started it. We were shocked when the Bill took us out of the cell and said, "You're being picked up, the RAF police are coming to get you."

To cut a long story short, we were all taken to camp where a high ranking officer gave us the seeing to, and told us this was serious and the book would be thrown at us. They had wanted to get us lot for a long time and stupid us had just given them their bullets. There is a little known law of this land that has never been repealed: spies, treason and piracy are all still hanging offences, and the local civvy cops and lawyers wanted us all to be done under the piracy law.

Wow, it didn't take any of us long to admit to all the offences; they were not fucking about the Queen's Rivers, Canals, and lakes and controlled UK seaways still has the piracy law, and although we probably would not be hung, (gulp) but still be punished. Well times like this you have to be sensible and hold your hands up, on one of the occasions we all had a meal together outside our cells and we all agreed to admit and told our appointed lawyer we would plead guilty to all.

This was a good thing as now it would not go to a court martial, we would accept punishment handed out from camp, and would not have to attend a civvy court as well which, on occasions it happened, we got put inside a military prison and spent some time each being shouted at and treated like shit. Our mates from civvy world were also done: one who had previous and an outstanding warrant went to prison for six months, the others were done for theft (the girls) and for fighting, also being drunk in charge of a boat on the waterways (well you live and learn). We four were also told we would never, ever be allowed to hire a boat, ship or any water carrying vehicle on the rivers, canals and seas of this country. Well I'll stick to swimming anyway and good old Terra Firma.

Taxi Home

I don't drink now and, just before I'd stopped drinking, my nights out had slowed anyway. Age, it gets us all, and I get fed-up not being around Skins when I'm out. I'm not having a go at all the people I hang around with, but I'm a Skin and I do like talking Skin with Skins. There are not many around now in Reading.

Anyway, I'd been out and had a good night, was very pissed and now the time to get home had come. I wasn't going to catch a bus, as that meant a stroll into town and a wait, so the taxi rank was just over the road and looked very enticing. Over I walked, or staggered, and by luck straight into a cab – like most cabbies in Reading, an Asian driver. Even though there were not many Skins about now, he did a double take as I got in and he somehow understood my pissed-up speech and where I wanted to go.

Vroom – off we went: the usual cabby speech, long day – when you finishing – yarda, yarda. Then as we went along, all I heard was "Oh no, oh no, no!"

I came out of my beer-induced trance to see what the driver was oh-noing about. In front of us was a bus blocking the road, and just in front of that was a car, side on and very dented. It seemed the car had lost a thumping competition with the bus and the road was blocked.

" I need to take a different route," the driver said.

"Good idea – this is going to be ages before it clears," I slurred.

He started to turn and then I heard horns blaring, the brakes were slammed on and I was thrown across the cab interior.

"Fucking hell!" I shouted, then noticed the driver was in an argument with another taxi firm driver, also an Asian. Fuck knows what they were going on about, but both pointing at each other and both irate.

He pulled his head back into the cab and said, "Sorry sir, I will continue the journey. This idiot hasn't a clue how to drive."

Okay, I thought, but it was funny watching them have a set to.

No more problems – a normal drive to where I told him to drop me off. "Here will do, mate."

We stopped, he told me how much and I dug through my pockets for the cash. Then, without any warning, his driver's door was kicked and I heard shouting. The driver looked out the window and straightaway was saying something on the radio in a panicked voice. The door was opened and he was pulled out, being thumped and shouted at in a foreign tongue. It seemed, as he dropped me off, the bod he'd had an argument with had dropped off someone just over the road, and now he wanted to carry on the argument as well as dishing out some aggravation. The bloke who had attacked also shouted something at me. What the fuck had I done? All I wanted was a quiet journey home in a cab to sleep off the booze. Anyway the switch had been clicked.

I got out of the door on the opposite side of the car and, as I did, I noticed a bit of fencing the local junior idiots had pulled off a fence. It was just lying there, oh yes. I picked it up and went round the cab. My driver was on the floor getting the shit punched out of him and the one who was attacking him just looked up. I swung my bit of wood at him – SMASH! – straight across his looking up face, straight down the middle, from forehead, across his nose and mouth. A gurgle and then nothing. He was out for the count. My bit of fence also broke and, just as I was going to put the boot in, my little driver just said, "Thank you, thank you," and was hanging onto my leg. This caught me cold. I hadn't even had time to yell abuse at the twat who had shouted at me and also attacked my driver. Fuck – how could I swing a leg now?

Then, from nowhere, cars pulled up, more taxis. OH FUCK, I

thought, I'm going to get a kicking now. About six Asian blokes jumped out of the cars and ran to my driver, who by now was standing next to me, bleeding from mouth and nose and not looking very good. They stopped looked at me and looked at the driver. I didn't know who they'd come to help, but thank the gods they were his mates. He said something to them and they patted me on my shoulders and then started to kick the other bloke on the ground. I was shocked (me, a Skin?). That was going to be my finale before I strolled on home.

The little driver who I'd helped said, "Sorry sir. This is a cabby firm argument. We will sort it now."

I had to ask, "How much was the fare, mate?"

He looked at me and said, "Maybe next time?" and smiled through his bloody face.

Well, there was another shock – you cannot get much from these fellas for free, but I suppose I did do him a favour. So I gathered this set to had been going on for a while – a family firm split into two and were at war with each other over who was the number one cabby co. I don't know who won. I just catch a cab every now and then, but I've never ever seen the bloke I clobbered with the fence. I've seen the other one, and I think he recognises me, but hey – WE ALL LOOK THE SAME DON'T WE?!

The Odd Conversation

2013: A Wednesday in April, and it was my birthday: the plan for that day was to go down town and have a coffee and chat with my eldest daughter, to go about 10ish in the morning, so I didn't have to push and shove with the mass ranks of ignorant shoppers that invade the town centre every day.

As I was waiting for the bus (a rarity, I hate buses), an old coloured guy in his late sixties joined me on the communal waiting seats. From the corner of my eye I could see him looking me up and down. Oh dear, I thought, I'm gonna have the usual racist argument. I didn't look at him; I waited for the bus and got on. I found an empty seat (the bus was empty) and sat by the window. The black guy came along and plonked himself next to me. Here we go, I thought.

"Hi, I'm Roger. You don't mind me talking to you?"

I looked at him and said, trying not to be confrontational or disrespectful, "No mate, I don't, but what's up?"

"Nothing. You're a skinhead aren't you, and you ain't young?" he said in a VERY STRONG Caribbean accent, not like the crap the young black youths try nowadays – you can tell the difference. He held out his hand and wanted a handshake. Okay, I thought. I'll shake it; he will either be very sincere or try a punch or head butt. We shook hands.

"Like I said, I'm Roger."

"And I'm Spike."

Well that seemed to go down okay – broke the ice. He asked me if I was off to work. I told him no, it's my birthday and am off to have a coffee with my daughter. He chuckled at that and said something like, am I not having a drink? I told him I haven't had a drink for about five years. I'm not allowed to drink any more; I abused it too much, and now it could kill me. Another chuckle and he said the same with him, "The rum. It was the rum."

That made me laugh. He then told me he is only in England for a month, visiting family then going back home. "TOO COLD, BONES CAN'T TAKE THE COLD," he tells me. He used to live in England and moved to London with his parents in the 50s. We have a chat. He asks how long have I been a Skin. I tell him since 1977 and how old I was, which makes him chuckle again. He then comes out with a surprise.

"I WAS A SKINHEAD IN THE LATE 60s EARLY 70s," he tells me.

That got us really chatting. We talk about the skinhead scene as of then and now. I tell him about my elder brother who was an original as well, how politics had ruined the cult and how the music had changed, how the Skins had adopted the Punk music into it, etc. He didn't like Punk – too noisy, he said. We chat about the Ska, bluebeat, skinhead reggae, and how it's coming back large now, and how I love Laurel Aitken. He tells me his favourites and we get to chat about clothes and his enemies of the time, which shocked me: bikers, teds, Rockers, even an odd fight at football with other Skins, were his number one hates. He then says, "Also Rude Boys."

Puzzled look on my face. "What do you mean?" I asked.

"People get it wrong. We were black Skins. Skinheads like the white boys, our friends. Rudies were different; bad boys they were, taken the name from the gangs back home, not Skins. Can't see how the name got mixed up. The ones that got called that usually went round with Mods, dressed like Mods, but always had crewcut hair, and crossed over music, Ska and the Mod music."

This was a shock. I never heard a black Skin or ex black Skin explain that. He was adamant they (Rude Boys) were not Skins. He said that they would argue with and even fight the Rude Boys of the time. He said his Mum and Dad used to say, "You're not going round with

Rude Boys. You hang around with them, you get a belt."

That made me laugh as well. Okay being a Skin, but not a Rude Boy.

We had a good chat on the forty minutes into town. As we got near my stop, I shook his hand again and wished him well. As I was to get off the bus he says,

"It's the music, Spike. It's all about the music. The clothes and attitude go with the music. When it dies, we die."

What a great old bloke. I love talking to, but very rarely meet with, black originals. The thing is they are just like the white Skins of that earlier time: same attitude, same likes and the love for music. We could all learn a lot from them; politics and shit meant nothing. It was all about being loyal to friends and the love of music and having a laugh.

Cheers Roger, my friend.

Today and Now

Today and now, what's changed? Well, I'm older, well into my 50s. I don't stand in town centres on street corners any more. For a start I'd get nicked for being some sort of old nutter or something, and it's just not the thing to do any more. I do go to those big coffee shops in the town centre and sit for an hour or two, sup the many concoctions of blends of coffee, and chat to my son (the Mod), but I never see any other Skins Punks or Mods; in fact no other old sub culture, not my age or younger. Nobody wants to make the effort to arrange to meet up, or really wants to anyway, and the radio and TV doesn't have countless Ska, Skinhead reggae or even Two tone playing. It's only our memories and gigs that keep it going. Yes there are the odd DJs that do their gigs for our pleasure, but they're few and far between. Reading is not the centre of Skin city like it used to be. Kids nowadays would rather take drugs and be a twopenny rapping acting gangztar.

Another problem is money. When I lost my job after an accident at work, I had a few years of hospitals and operations on my back and legs; then when I got fitter and tried for jobs, I've just been turned away. They don't take notice of my experience or job history, they just look at my sick record, related working time and accident details. I get my coat straight away, and now I don't even get any interviews, as these days the world is run by the Net; you apply online and get nothing back. It seems the employment world have not got the balls to even see people any more and say no, they just press delete. It seems I am destined to spend what's left of my life dreaming of a job instead of working. So going out happens very seldom and when I do it's lucky I don't drink, 'cause WOW – the beers have gone up in price – another rip-off for the working man. Those in charge have really got us all by the bollocks. I do see a few friends on the odd occasion out; most of them are younger by a few years, but all are well into the scooter and Mod scene, so we have a good chat and have some things in common, but I still feel on the outside. I have no money or work and I think they all know that. But hey, there is always *The Wasters* and their blend of Punk, Mod, Rock and fun. Thanks to Rod and Co.

What does get on my wick is: when I'm standing at the Wasters' gigs, or anywhere, and I'll get somebody who knew me long ago or just wants to talk. They see me as some sort of fascination. I will guarantee within the first minutes they will say, "Oh, I had a row with my boss about (some foreigner or coloured person) and told him straight." Why the fuck do I wanna know – is that all you have to go on about after years of not seeing me? When they look at me, is all they see an SS officer in black uniform and wearing a swastika? I know it's our fault (skinhead and mine for my past) for the bad press of the late 70s and 80s, but for fuck's sake give me the benefit. I just have to look at them, take a breath and wish them luck. They have no idea.

I've also tried to find old friends: Skins, Mods, Punks et al. That's the good thing about the Net. Many are on Facebook or other social sites but, boy do you get a shock? Some people have short memories or are very much in denial. It's easy to say hello on the Internet – they don't have to look at you. These people will just pretend they were never there. I'll not say who, but recently, after many months of trying and searching, I came across a girl I've been looking for to talk about old times and ask her for contact to another girl I have also been seeking for years. She was good friends with her and I'd like to get in touch with her again. Fuck me! I've never been so shocked. She basically denied being part of our mob; she denied ever doing anything wrong and slandered other people I'd asked her about. She gave the excuse they were all small-minded fools – yarda-yarda.

Well my dear, I think you're the problem. I told her that. I just wanted contact details – all I wanted was a chat with who I thought was an old friend, and some info. I got denial and hate from her. Maybe I should have put in this book some of the things I did when she was about, and she took part in. That would change her standing and the way her now friends think of her. But I'm not bitter and twisted. I'm the one who moved on. She is the one, like others, with a denial problem. Again I wished her luck and may your gods go with you. I do get down when I find out so many of my old friends have died through drugs or are addicts now. Why? Most were not stupid and they knew the risk. What makes it worse is that most all have kids and they have gone the same way: generations of drug users, and they see nothing wrong in this. There is no body of officials changing this. I do hate the term "we grew up" Yeah, I know what they mean, but let's face it – when they stopped the sub culture they were into, they joined a bigger one – the general public – they just don't see it. But I must say I too have; I don't think the same way, I don't act the same way. Maybe I got wise. That's what my daughter tells me; it shows with the grey in my lamb chops.

Do I like being a Skin? Oh yes. Do I miss the old days? Yep, and all the old friends, and all the bad things I did and saw. I wouldn't do them again, but I'll never forget and some things I'll never tell. Will I stay a Skin. NO, age catches us all. 2017 will give me 40 years. Duty done then I think, but then it's wearing the loafers and jeans, only a belt instead of braces, and keep the sheepskin and Crombie on the streets until they are threadbare and faded, just like me – threadbare and fading out.

Maybe the music will always be there, its history and hopefully someone to play it, and there will always be a few that take the Skin scene to heart, keep it going, as it was the first time round – the weak and the posers will fall away – what's left will be the heart and soul of a sub culture that has been a part of this country's youth history. Dump the politics and reinstall the movement from its inception: MUSIC,

GIRLS, DANCING, BEER, AND THE ODD FIGHT... SKIN-HEAD!

Spike Pitt

Now, with granddaughter, Aubree...

Lightning Source UK Ltd.
Milton Keynes UK
UKHW010945100720
366326UK00002B/638